OLIVE OIL

OLIVE OIL

A GUIDE TO SELECTING AND USING THE WORLD'S MOST VERSATILE SUPER-FOOD

TINA and GARETH LOFTHOUSE

Arcturus Publishing Limited
26/27 Bickels Yard
151–153 Bermondsey Street
London SE1 3HA

Published in association with
foulsham
W. Foulsham & Co. Ltd,
The Publishing House, Bennetts Close, Cippenham,
Slough, Berkshire SL1 5AP, England

ISBN: 978-0-572-03401-6

This edition printed in 2007

British Library Cataloguing-in-Publication Data: a catalogue record for this book is available from the British Library

Illustrations by Madeleine Davis

Printed in China

Introduction

There has always been something almost magical about olive oil. From the dawn of civilization, the green-gold extract from the bitter fruit of the olive tree has been prized as much for its health-giving properties as its culinary qualities and versatility.

Nothing evokes the sun-drenched tastes and aromas of the Mediterranean like olive oil. What other ingredient can transform the humblest of foods – a slab of crusty bread, a handful of ripe tomatoes, a few slivers of rustic cheese – into a fresh and alluring supper? With its unique depth of flavour, olive oil is the foundation of some of the world's greatest cuisines. Just try imagining Italian pasta, Spanish paella or a simple French dressing without it, and you realize what a dreary place the world would be without olive oil.

Unlike many other cooking fats, which are greasy and unappetizing on their own, good olive oil has a cleanness and depth of flavour that allows it to be savoured straight from the bottle. As a result, it is as good drizzled 'raw' over a simple char-grilled fish as it is added to a hearty stew or used as a base for a classic Italian sauce.

Moreover, no two olive oils are exactly alike. Olive oil offers a huge diversity of different styles and flavours, ranging from the light and delicate through to the more fruity

and robust. Judging the quality of these oils is a serious business, with professional experts assessing each product by its colour, bouquet and taste. To properly savour the best oils – some of which command a price once reserved for fine wines – it is important to carefully match the style and flavour of the oil to the type of dish desired. Knowing what characteristics and qualities to look for is half the secret of getting the most out of olive oil. The rest comes down to how you use it, and how you look after it.

Olive oil offers a huge diversity of different styles and flavours, ranging from the light and delicate through to the more fruity and robust

Olive oil has been used for centuries as a medicine, as a fuel in oil lamps, for religious, ceremonial and decorative purposes

Of course, olive oil has always been more than just another cooking fat. A vitally important commodity for early civilizations, it has been used for centuries as a medicine, as a fuel in oil lamps, for religious, ceremonial and decorative purposes – even as a sexual lubricant! And while some of these uses are less common in the modern world, it certainly seems that the ancients were right to attribute life-giving properties to olive oil. A growing body of scientific evidence suggests that olive oil brings many health-

related benefits, and that in particular it can help to reduce the risk of coronary heart disease when consumed as part of a balanced diet. So, as well as exploring how olive oil can please the palate, this book also looks at how it can contribute to a healthier lifestyle in general.

Fortunately, it is now almost as easy to enjoy olive oil in the chillier states of North America as it is on a sun-baked Greek island. Most large supermarkets stock a wide selection of olive oils, ranging from the most basic to the highest-quality artisan products. But with such a bewildering array of choice on offer, consumers can be forgiven for being confused when it comes to knowing what to buy. What qualities make a great and long-lasting olive oil? Which countries and producers offer the best oils, and for what purposes? This book provides an introduction to the fascinating world of olive oil, and aims to help readers get the most from this healthy and increasingly popular product.

Olive oil and the ancients

Native to the Mediterranean basin, the olive tree is among the oldest cultivated fruit trees and one which has had a unique impact on human history. But its precise origins are unclear.

Most experts believe that the cultivated olive tree originated in Asia Minor in about 6000 BCE, somewhere between present-day Syria and Iran. From there it spread to Greece, where systematic techniques for cultivation were developed. In Crete, archaeologists have found huge amphorae that were used to store and transport olive oil, which suggests that it was already a valuable commodity in Greece by the 2nd millennium BCE.

Olive oil has also been found in Egyptian tombs, including that of Tutankhamun

In time, olive oil assumed a huge importance in Greek culture. It was a major Greek export, and ships were constructed specifically to transport the oil from Greece to outposts around the Mediterranean. Increasingly, it became a source of wealth and power: such was its value that the poet Homer described it as 'liquid gold'. It was held in such reverence that the Greeks even deemed their olive groves as sacred ground, and only virgins and chaste men were allowed to cultivate them. Anyone who dared commit the heinous crime of cutting an olive tree down could be condemned to exile or even death.

Its usefulness in cooking as well as its versatility for a wide range of other purposes caused olive oil to spread throughout the Mediterranean basin. With the expansion of the Greek colonies, olive oil culture reached southern Italy and northern Africa in the 8th century BCE. Olive oil has also been found in Egyptian tombs, including that of Tutankhamun. It was used in Ancient Egypt for oil lamps, as well as for anointing the dead and for other religious purposes.

The Spartans are believed to have been the first to use olive oil for decorative purposes. Athletes anointed themselves with it while exercising in the gymnasia in the belief that it highlighted the beauty of the male body. From there the practice spread to all of Greece, and the belief that it conferred strength and youth became widespread in many ancient civilizations. In Egypt and Rome as well as Greece, it was combined with flowers and herbs to produce medicinal and cosmetic ointments. Archaeologists have even found the remains of an ancient perfume factory in Cyprus, where olive oil was again combined with herbs to create appealing fragrances.

Sustaining the might of Rome

The olive tree's cultivation in Italy is thought to have started in the 7th century BCE during the reign of Lucius Tarquinius Priscus, the fifth king of Rome. Olive oil became an important economic commodity for the Roman Empire, the expansion of which acted as a catalyst for the wider spread of olive tree cultivation.

Roman taxes were often paid in the form of oil tributes sent to the imperial city. Given its prominence in the economy of Rome, it is not surprising that the Romans introduced improvements to the cultivation, pruning, harvesting, production and storage of the olive tree and oil. Cato, the great Roman statesman and orator, wrote extensively on these procedures and the uses of olive oil in *De Agri Cultura*, one of the earliest surviving works of Latin literature. The Romans also began to carefully grade oil by quality: *Olei Floris*, which means 'the flower of the oil', was the equivalent of today's extra virgin olive oil, being produced solely from the first pressing of the olives.

The olive tree arrived in Marseilles around 600 BCE, and from there it spread to the whole of Gaul. In Spain, the olive was

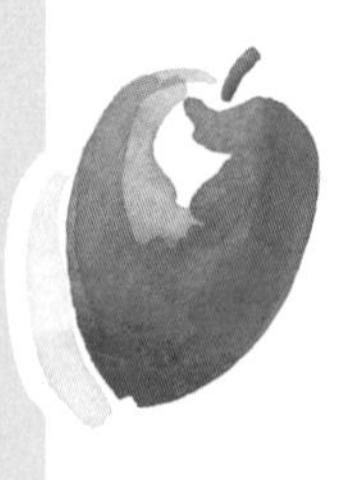

originally introduced by the Phoenicians (1050 BCE), but large-scale cultivation came about under Roman rule. Later, the Arabs introduced their own varieties to the south of Spain. Their influence can be detected in the Spanish words for olive (*aceituna*), oil (*aceite*), and wild olive tree (*acebuche*), which have Arabic roots.

The collapse of the Roman Empire represented a setback for the advance of the olive. The scale of cultivation diminished and it was not until the Renaissance in Europe that it fully revived. But by the 16th century, the olive had become widespread in areas of Italy and Spain.

Roman taxes were often paid in the form of oil tributes sent to the imperial city

Sacred fruit: the olive in myth and religion

The olive holds a uniquely symbolic position in the myths and religions of many cultures.

In Greek mythology, the origins of Athens are inextricably intertwined with the olive tree. According to one myth, Athens was built by the semi-god Cecrope, who was half man and half snake. As the first king, Cecrope unified the populations of the Attic villages of the Acropolis and asked the gods for a sign of their protection.

Pallas Athena, daughter of Zeus, and Poseidon, the god of the sea, competed to come up with the best sign and for the right to confer their name on the city. Poseidon struck a rock with his trident, unleashing a torrent of seawater and a horse that could run faster than the wind. Athena's creation was less dramatic but infinitely more useful: she planted the first olive tree, a source of food, healing and light for the people of the new city state. Having won the competition, Athena became the city's protector and namesake. To honour her, the Greeks chose to build the Parthenon very near to this legendary first olive tree.

The olive also has great significance in the major religious texts. In

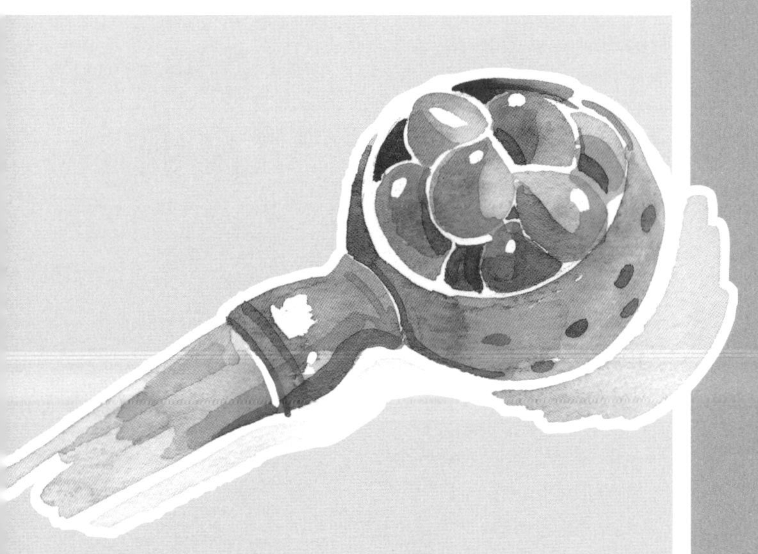

the Bible, the Book of Genesis tells how Noah waited seven days after the great flood before freeing a dove. The dove returned with an olive branch in its beak, signalling that God had made peace with man. To this day, people speak of 'offering an olive branch' when seeking to resolve conflict.

The Koran makes numerous mentions of the olive tree. The Prophet of Islam, Muhammad, advised his followers to apply olive oil to their bodies, and used olive oil on his own head.

Olive oil's preciousness and symbolic importance is also reflected in its use throughout history for ceremonial purposes. Historically, olive oil was used to anoint kings and queens at their coronation. Even today, the Catholic and Orthodox Churches still use olive oil for the Oil of Catechumens, which plays a part in baptisms. It is also the basis for Sacred Chrism, which is used to consecrate altars and churches as part of confirmations and for the ordination of priests.

The olive reaches the New World

Olive oil arrived in the New World with the Spanish Conquistadors at the beginning of the 16th century. The first olive trees were shipped from Seville to the West Indies and later to the American continent. Regular production of olive groves began in Mexico towards the end of the 16th century, and from here expanded to Peru and Chile. At about the same time the plant was introduced in Argentina. In the Arauco region in northern Argentina, there is an old olive tree called 'Olivo de Arauco' that was planted when Charles III was king of Spain.

According to some sources, the olive tree was introduced to California in the 18th century by Fray Junípero Serra, founder of the San Diego de Alcalá mission. The Franciscan fathers planted olives in the missions they established along the Californian coast. The Mission olive, now grown throughout California, takes its name from these beginnings.

Olive oil today

Olive oil has grown into a huge industry, which is today a source of income for over 12 million people around the world.

Production is still concentrated in the Mediterranean basin, with Spain, Portugal, Italy, Greece, Turkey, Tunisia and Morocco alone accounting for 90 per cent of the world's output. But the olive tree has spread far and wide to new regions including the Americas and, more recently, southern Africa, Australia, Japan and China.

Perhaps not surprisingly, it is in the olive oil heartlands of the Mediterranean where people are most likely to consume large

quantities of olive oil – the average Greek gets through an astonishing 24 litres a year!

By comparison, consumers in northern Europe and in the wider world have some catching up to do. But there is no doubt that good olive oil is becoming accessible – and increasingly appreciated – in more parts of the world. Moreover, as new markets have opened up for olive oil, a number of New World producers are producing oils that can compete with the best European product, in terms of flavour if not quantity. This, combined with stronger regulation of quality and technological improvements to the production and storage, means that we can look forward to an even greater choice of good quality olive oils in the years ahead.

The average Greek gets through an astonishing 24 litres of olive oil a year

The olive tree

The olive tree's proliferation around the world can be attributed to its astonishing toughness and adaptability. The tree has famous longevity – some are believed to be well over 1,000 years old, while most endure for about 500 years.

There are thousands of different varieties – or cultivars – of olive tree to be found around the world. But they share some common characteristics

Many varieties can thrive in dry and inhospitable environments, a fact which has helped the peoples of the Mediterranean to turn even the most unpromising strips of earth into productive land. The trees are also renowned for their almost miraculous resilience – even when chopped to the ground an olive tree can quickly sprout back again.

That the olive is a tree at all is largely down to mankind's influence. Look at a wild olive, and you will find a small, spiny shrub. It was only after thousands of years of cultivation and selection that the olive became the tree we recognize today.

There are thousands of different varieties – or cultivars – of olive tree to be found around the world. But they share some common characteristics. The tree is an attractive evergreen with grey-green foliage and distinctive gnarled branches. Untended, they grow to approximately 15m/50ft in height, but they are generally kept to about 6m/20ft through periodic pruning.

The small cream-coloured flowers of the olive tree usually blossom in April and May in the Mediterranean, and are a good indication of the ultimate crop size. The flowers are mainly wind-pollinated and most varieties can self-pollinate, but cross-pollination with other cultivars is often beneficial for producing better fruit yields. Several varieties cannot self-pollinate and therefore only produce fruit when they are inter-planted with other varieties.

Technically the olive fruit itself is a green drupe (a fleshy fruit with a single hard stone that encloses a seed). Most olives gradually ripen from a pastel green to dark green, then violet, finally reaching a blackish-purple when fully ripe. There are a few varieties that are green when ripe and some which ripen to a copper brown.

The olive tree can grow well in nutrient-poor soil, but it needs a long, hot growing season to properly ripen the fruit

The size of the olive fruit is variable, even on the same tree. Raw olives contain an alkaloid that in most cases makes them bitter and unpalatable, so various chemical treatments are used to make them suitable as table olives that can be eaten. However, a few varieties are sufficiently sweet to be eaten after drying in the sun.

The olive tree can grow well in nutrient-poor soil, but it needs a long, hot growing season to properly ripen the fruit. A slight winter chill is also required to ensure that the trees produce a good quantity of fruit, but late spring frosts can kill the blossoms and can therefore be a problem in olive-growing areas with colder winters, such as Tuscany and Provence. Olive trees should not be planted in areas where the temperature falls below -5°C (23°F).

Rainfall is another factor that can affect the olive's fruit yield. The olive tree can produce satisfactory yields in low-rainfall areas, providing that it is planted in soil with good water-retaining capacity. In high-rainfall areas, producers can still achieve a good olive yield providing adequate drainage is in place. While olives are extremely drought-tolerant, irrigation systems are sometimes used to ensure that the trees bear a good volume of fruit. But despite the olive tree's adaptability and the attempts to manage the impact of either droughts or frosts, the weather can still, of course, have a major impact on olive oil production.

A further factor that producers must contend with is that most olive trees tend toward biennial cropping. This means that they produce a big harvest one year and a small one the next. This creates particular challenges for the industry: obviously a smaller harvest means less money for producers, but bumper crops also cause problems because the producer must race to harvest a large amount of olives in a brief period of time to ensure that their quality is preserved. Fortunately, pruning and irrigation can help producers limit the effects of biennial cropping to some degree.

Green and black olives

As well as producing oil, the olive itself is a prominent feature of Mediterranean cuisine – whether it comes as the perfect appetizer in the form of a bowl of marinated olives, or as an ingredient in pizzas, pasta dishes, salads, tagines or a multitude of other dishes. And as with olive oil, the appetite for table olives is rising elsewhere in the world – US consumers alone nibble through over 200,000 tonnes of them a year.

Most table olives have to be cured before they are suitable for consumption. Olives that are good for producing oil are not necessarily the best for making table olives – in fact, generally, fruits with low oil content make better table olives, although some black olives benefit from a higher oil content. A few varieties such as Mission and Picholine are grown to make both oil and table olives.

Methods for treating table olives vary from region to region. Green olives are picked when they have reached full size but before they are ripe. They are processed in two principal ways: with fermentation (the Spanish style) and without fermentation (a style popular in France and

Green olives are picked when they have reached full size but before they are ripe

America). Spanish varieties such as Manzanillo are immersed in sodium hydroxide to remove their bitterness.

Fermentation is then carried out in suitable containers – traditionally wooden casts – in which the olives are covered with brine. By contrast, the French and the Americans tend to soak the fruit in brine first, then in sodium hydroxide, using regular changes of water to disperse the bitterness. Black olives are ripe fruits that are soaked in brine, often pricked so that the salt penetrates them, thus acting as a preservative. Greek olives such as Kalamata are prepared in this fashion.

Olive cultivars: thousands of varieties, a multitude of flavours

The choice of olive variety is one of the biggest factors determining the quality and flavour of each olive oil. There are thousands of varieties, or cultivars, of olive tree worldwide, each suited to different climates and environments, and every type produces an oil with its own unique properties.

Many producers blend different varietals together to produce a well-balanced oil, but there has also been a trend towards single varietal oils, just as we have seen increased popularity for single varietal wines from the New World. Of course, some varieties work better on their own than others.

Although there are thousands of different cultivars, the majority of olives come from a number of leading varieties that have become widely adopted in a particular country. Although each variety has distinct characteristics, the flavours of these oils also vary significantly depending on other factors. These include the ripeness and health of the olive when they are picked, the impact of climate and (to a lesser degree) the 'terroir' – in other words, the unique qualities of the soil and local environment.

Arbequina

The Arbequina variety comes from Catalonia, but it is now being planted in other olive-growing regions in Spain and in other olive-producing countries. The tree is fairly vigorous and has a medium-sized crown. Its popularity is boosted by the fact that it is small enough to be suited to dense planting, but it still yields a good amount of oil. It is also self-fertile and there is no tendency to biennial cropping. In Spain there are about 10,000 hectares of Arbequina olive groves.

Olive oil from this variety is fresh and fruity, often with hints of apple and green grass. It is neither very bitter nor pungent, and has a sweet flavour. It is a smooth olive oil that is very fluid in the mouth, and often exhibits flavours redolent of almond and fresh-cut grass. It has average to low stability, making its shelf-life shorter than oils from some other popular varieties.

Coratina

Coratina olives are cultivated mainly in Puglia and other southern provinces of Italy. The tree is of medium size with a globe-shaped crown, and it produces large olives. It yields a high proportion of high-quality oil, and is fairly resistant to both drought and cold.

Coratina olive oils are very fruity, with a fragrance of apple and green leaves. They are bitter and pungent, with some astringency and sweetness. They have a well-balanced flavour that is reminiscent of artichokes and aromatic herbs. Coratina oils are also highly stable.

Cornicabra

This variety is primarily found in central Spain, in the Castilian region of La Mancha, where there are over 250,000 hectares of olive groves. The tree is upright with medium-length branches. The olives ripen late, usually starting at the end of October and finishing in January.

Olive oil obtained from the Cornicabra olive variety has a medium to high olive fruity flavour and is strongly aromatic. When picked early, the olives produce a fresh oil that tends to be very smooth on the palate, with notes of almond. Late-harvest olives are lightly bitter and have a flavour of exotic fruits. Cornicabra produces one of the most stable oils. It can be kept for about a year after pressing, a fact which helps make this variety a popular choice for blending.

Frantoio

Originating in Tuscany, this is now one of the most popular olive varieties worldwide because of its vigorous nature and its tendency to produce oil of a high quality. It is extremely popular in Italy, where it occupies 100,000 hectares and is predominantly found in

central areas, including the regions of Tuscany, Le Marche and Umbria.

In the cooler climate of Tuscany the fruit matures slowly to a purple-black colour, but the preferred picking time is usually earlier in the year when the olives are green and purple. Harvesting the olives at this stage results in an oil that is very fruity, notably with hints of green apple and the scent of green leaves and grass.

Galega

The Galega olive is the main variety grown in Portugal, and it is used exclusively to make olive oil. It is a robust cultivar, which can withstand quite tough conditions.

It produces a small olive with an oil that is fruity and grassy. The oil is pungent and slightly bitter with a sweet taste, and is moderately long-lasting. Some experts believe it produces better oils when blended with other varieties.

Hojiblanca

Another major Spanish variety – there are currently 220,000 hectares planted in the provinces of Cordoba, Granada, Malaga and Seville. The Hojiblanca is a vigorous tree with an average-size crown and dense foliage. The name means 'white leaf' and refers to the colour on the back side of the leaves.

Hojiblanca olives produce an oil that is very balanced with an enormous range of flavours. There is a slight bitter taste, although sometimes the oil can be pungent and sweet. Hojiblanca olive oil is quite smooth and feels light in the mouth with an almondy aftertaste. The oil is not particularly long-lasting but is otherwise well regarded.

Cornicabra produces one of the most stable oils. It can be kept for about a year after pressing

Koroneiki

This is the most widely planted olive tree in Greece and is certainly the most important in terms of the production of olive oil. It is cultivated on the island of Crete, in Messenia and Zante.

The Koroneiki tree is fairly vigorous. It copes well with drought, but is more susceptible to cold weather. The small fruit ripens early and produces a consistently high proportion of oil which is very fruity and quite peppery. The oil is well balanced and reveals hints of almond, fig and bark in the mouth. It is also one of the longer-lasting oils available.

Leccino

Leccino olives are grown throughout the major olive-growing regions of Italy, and Leccino is one of the most important cultivars in the country. Its popularity partly stems from the fact that it quickly produces fruit and is resistant to parasites and adverse climates. The variety is self-sterile and so needs a pollinator – Pendolino or Maurino are principally used for this purpose. The fruit has a variable oil content of between 16 and 21 per cent.

Leccino olive oil is mild, sweet and has a delicate fruitiness. It tends to be a lightly coloured oil with average stability.

Mission
The name of this olive variety originates from the fact that it was established throughout California by the Franciscan missions. It is a dual-purpose variety that is used for green and black table olives as well as to produce oil. The tree is only moderately productive and the fruit ripens late. When mature, the olives produce about 22 per cent oil content.

The olive oil derived from this variety shows a good level of olive fruitiness, with hints of green apple. It is pungent and sweet, with a very noticeable flavour of almonds. The oil has average stability.

Moraiolo
This is a resilient Italian variety that has been widely planted in the regions of Tuscany, Umbria, Le Marche and Abruzzo. The fruit is quite small, and has consistently high oil content.

Olive oils from Moraiolo tend to be powerfully fruity and herbaceous. They are slightly bitter and pungent, but also have a sweetness on the palate. A good oil, but low stability means that it is not particularly long-lasting.

Picholine
This is the main variety planted in France, and it is used for both table olives and oil. The tree is fairly vigorous and is known to be a good producer that can adapt to various climates and soils. For that reason, it is increasingly becoming a popular cultivar in other parts of the world.

The oil produced from this variety tends to have a golden colour with hints of green spiciness. It is a mild and sweet oil. Its aroma is ripe and fruity and it has a smooth texture on the palate.

Picholine Marocaine
This is the predominant variety in Morocco, the seventh largest olive-producing nation. The olives from this variety are used both for table olives and oil.

It produces an oil that is intensely fruity, bitter and pungent with a leafy aroma. It also has a distinctive taste of figs and bark, and is averagely stable.

Picual
The most widely planted variety in the world, the Picual accounts for 50 per cent of Spain's olives

and 20 per cent worldwide. It is linked to Andalusia, the main olive-producing region in the world, and especially to Jaen, Cordoba and Granada. However, due to its popularity, Picual olives are now cultivated in other olive-producing countries as well as all around Spain.

The Picual variety is extremely vigorous and robust with short, spreading branches. The tree starts to produce early and is highly productive, a factor that has contributed to its popularity. It also adapts well to different climatic and soil conditions and can tolerate frost – although it has limited resistance to drought.

Olive oil from Picual olives has a strong and distinctive character. It has an intense olive fruitiness with a bitter and pungent taste. It is also noted for flavours that are reminiscent of fig and wet bark. With its high stability, olive oil from the Picual variety can be enjoyed for an unusually long period of time after pressing.

Major olive cultivars

CULTIVAR	AVERAGE % OIL FROM FRUIT	HARDINESS	FRUIT SIZE
Arbequina	20-22	Hardy	Small
Coratina	21-26	Hardy	Medium
Cornicabra	23-27	Hardy	Medium
Frantoio	17-22	Sensitive	Medium
Galega	14-18	Hardy	Small
Hojiblanca	17-19	Hardy	Large
Koroneiki	24-26	Sensitive	Very small
Leccino	17-22	Hardy	Medium
Mission	21-22	Hardy	Medium
Moraiolo	17-24	Sensitive	Small
Picual	23-28	Hardy	Medium
Picudo	22-27	Hardy	Large
Picholine	18-20	Moderate	Medium
Picholine Marocaine	22-25	Hardy	Medium

OIL CHARACTERISTICS	STABILITY*	MAIN COUNTRY
Very fruity with slight apple taste, green grass, not very bitter or pungent, with a sweet flavour. Very fluid in the mouth.	Medium low	Spain
High level fruitiness, with slight hints of apple and green leaf aroma. Bitter, pungent and astringent with light sweetness.	High	Italy
Fruity, pungent, slightly bitter. Smooth on palate, often with a slight almond aftertaste.	Very high	Spain
Fruity, peppery oil, often with herbaceous notes and an almond finish.	Average	Italy
Fruity oil with green leaf and grass notes, lightly bitter and pungent with a sweet, almondy taste.	Average	Portugal
Wide-ranging flavours but often with notes of unripe fruit with light bitterness. Can be sweet and pungent, with nutty aftertaste.	Average	Spain
Produces very fruity, well-balanced oil. Hints of green apple, some aroma, bitter and pungent, with notes of almond, fig and bark.	Very high	Greece
Slightly fruity, light bitterness, somewhat sweet with a light, delicate colour.	Average	Italy
Fruity, peppery oil with a thick texture.	Average	US (California)
Good fruitiness, with bitterness and pungency balanced with sweet sensation on the palate. Almond flavour and grassy aroma.	Low	Italy
Intense olive fruitiness, highly aromatic, bitter, with distinctive hints of fig and wet bark.	Extremely high	Spain
A smooth oil, sometimes with notes of grass and exotic fruits.	Low	Spain
Mild, mellow and sweet, never bitter, fruity. Some oils offer a peppery bite.	Very high	France
Powerful olive fruitiness. Bitter and pungent. Fig and fresh bark flavours.	Average	Morocco

*The stability of the oil is the main factor in determining its shelf-life – the higher the stability, the longer the oil can be kept before it begins to deteriorate.

Olive cultivation today

Olive farming has moved on significantly from traditional practices, with modern growers using a variety of intensive farming techniques to produce a more reliable and abundant yield. Even today, however, cultivating olives requires patience.

It can take years of care and attention before an olive tree is ready to deliver a good harvest. The trees will begin to bear fruit typically after four or five years in the ground, but will not reach full production for 12 to 15 years.

Olive trees are usually grown from cuttings, a method which provides a more reliable replication of the parent tree than growing from seed. The cuttings are kept in a special kind of greenhouse for about four to six months until they sprout roots. They are then transplanted into pots, and after one year they are ready to go in the ground.

Traditionally olive orchards were sparsely planted, mainly because the trees had to grow on land that was dry and nutrient-poor. The olive tree's ability to survive in these conditions encouraged farmers to use the crop to bring marginal land under cultivation. However, modern farming techniques enable producers to plant orchards more densely and thereby to increase productivity. Although olive trees cope well with dry conditions, irrigation is widely used to maximize the fruit size and overall production, and it has the additional benefit of helping to reduce the tendency towards biennial cropping (see page 21). Fertilizers are also widely used to increase yields, and crops are sprayed with insecticides to control pests and diseases.

In recent years, however, the increased interest in organically grown foods has encouraged some producers to move in a different direction, in particular by avoiding the use of artificial fertilizers and pest controls. Organic oils tend to command a premium price in the market, and will normally be certified as organic on the label. However, the fact that an oil is made with organically grown olives does not necessarily mean that it will be of a high quality. Indeed, some experts argue that organic oil is often inferior, largely because in an organic plantation it is much more difficult to control pests and diseases that damage the quality of the fruit. Nevertheless, there is no doubt that a number of top-end producers are now making exceptionally good organic olive oils.

Organic oils tend to command a premium price in the market, and will normally be certified as organic on the label

Once the tree is old enough to be productive, pruning is used to encourage the growth of fruit-bearing branches

Pruning

Pruning plays an important role in ensuring that the olive tree is as productive and easy to cultivate and harvest as possible.

In the early stages of growth, pruning takes place to train the olive trees into a shape that allows easy access for spraying and harvesting. A variety of shapes are used in different parts of the Mediterranean, including the spherical cup shape found in France, Italy and Greece; the candlestick shape in Tunisia; and

the two or three trunk shape in Seville.

Once the tree is old enough to be productive, pruning is used to encourage the growth of fruit-bearing branches. The severity of the pruning required depends on the climate – olives grown in dry land need heavier pruning to ensure that any nutrients and water available are channelled into growing fruit. Proper pruning has the additional benefit of reducing the problems associated with biennial cropping. On intensively farmed plantations, mechanical pruning is often used to save labour.

Pruning can also be used to revitalize old or frost-damaged trees. One of the remarkable characteristics of the olive tree is that if you cut its wood it will produce new shoots. Old or low-yield trees can be completely rejuvenated by cutting the trunk at a low height; vigorous new shoots will sprout from the cut, which can then be trained to develop a new tree that will be ready to bear fruit again in three to five years.

Controlling pests and diseases

Damage caused by pests such as the olive fruit fly, olive moth and the black scale can cause major problems for producers.

The olive fruit fly can be found throughout the Mediterranean olive-growing countries, but not in the Americas or Australia. It lays its egg in the olive, which the larva feeds on. If the damaged olive is harvested, the larvae impart an unpleasant taste to the oil. Insecticides are commonly sprayed from the air to control the olive fruit fly. More environmentally friendly techniques are becoming more popular – for example, using pheromones to attract male olive flies so they can be killed before they have a chance to mate.

The olive moth is another problem for olive farmers, and it exists in all Mediterranean olive-growing countries. The moth feeds and develops on olive flowers, fruits and leaves. The main damage arises when its larvae eat into the kernel of the olive. Olive oil affected by the moth will have an oxidized and rancid taste.

Black scale is an insect that damages the olive tree by sucking its sap and depositing honeydew on to the leaves. This honeydew encourages the development of mould that can reduce photosynthesis and respiration, eventually causing leaves to drop. Pruning to create open trees discourages black scale infestation. Producers can also use

biological controls such as parasites and predators that attack black scale.

Olive farmers also have to protect their crops from several diseases, in particular verticillium wilt, olive knot and leaf spot. Verticillium wilt comes from a fungus that causes leaves on the olive tree to wilt early in the growing season. The disease spreads through the foliage and can eventually kill the tree. Treatments for verticillium wilt, once a tree is infected, are not always effective, so prevention tends to be the best course of action. Leaf spot is also caused by a fungus and is a particular problem in irrigated olive orchards or those where there is relatively high humidity. The undersides of leaves become discoloured and may fall off the tree, while the fruit develops brown spots and may not mature properly.

Olive knot is a bacterial disease that causes irregular bumps or 'knots' to appear on the olive trees branches. It does not kill trees, but can reduce productivity by destroying twigs and branches, and once again the flavour of the olive oil may be impaired.

Harvesting

The way a producer approaches harvesting can have a significant impact on the ultimate character and quality of the oil.

The timing of the harvest can be critical. Olives that are picked too early may contain very little oil. Allow them to ripen for too long, however, and the acidity levels in the oil will rise to the point where the final product is impaired. The optimum time for picking differs depending on the variety, and also to a certain extent on the style of oil that the producer is aiming for. For example, olives that are picked before being fully ripe tend to produce oil with a bitter, peppery flavour. By contrast, olives that are picked when fully ripe tend to result in a sweeter, milder oil.

Of course, it is easier for small olive estates to harvest all their olives at the optimal time than for larger operations. Large-scale producers often start harvesting the olives as soon as they contain a good amount of oil, and there may be as much as three to four months between picking the first olives and bringing in the last of the crop.

Harvesting olives is the most costly part of olive oil production. Many producers use picking machines, which shake the tree trunk and branches and catch the olives in nets as they fall. But mechanization has its drawbacks. When it comes to producing the best quality oils, traditional hand-picking is still preferable because it is the method that is least likely to cause damage to the fruit. Other manual methods include beating higher branches of the tree with poles to shake off the olives into nets, or using wooden or plastic tools to comb the fruit off the branches. Manual harvesting is extremely labour-intensive, so many producers restrict its use to areas where mechanization is not practical (for example, hilly slopes or sparsely planted areas). Limited hand picking is also used to collect fruit that the harvesting machines have missed.

Whichever harvesting method is employed, the producer must take every precaution to minimize damage to the olives. This is vital because any bruising or break in the skin of the fruit kicks off a process of deterioration that can lead to defects in the quality and taste of the oil. It is also important to mill the olives as quickly as possible after picking (usually within 24 hours).

The timing of the harvest can be critical – olives that are picked too early may contain very little oil

Extracting the oil

Once at the mill, it is time to extract the oil from the olives. The olives are first crushed in order to break down the cell structure of the fruit and thereby release the precious oil. The fruit is crushed whole, usually including the pit, which contains an important preservative. This process takes place after removing the leaves and any other possible contaminants, which could otherwise impair the flavour of the oil.

The traditional method uses millstones to crush the olives into a paste. Then the mash is pressed to separate the oil and vegetable water from the residual pulp (the 'pomace'). The mash is spread on mats which are stacked on top of each other, and then squeezed to release the oil. Historically this was done using a lever press (still employed in parts of northern Africa) or a screw press, but the hydraulic press is more common today. The traditional method can produce a very good quality oil, but it is extremely labour-intensive. It is also harder to keep the millstones and pressing equipment clean, which is vital to ensuring a good quality product.

Modern extraction mills use either metal grinders or hammer mills to crush the olives. Both are faster and more cost-effective than the traditional method. However, with some systems there is a risk that the olive paste will heat up during the process, and thus lose some of its delicate flavours. To label their oils as 'cold pressed' producers must ensure that temperatures during processing do not exceed 27°C (80°F).

An industrial centrifuge is used to separate the oil from the vegetable water and pulp. These systems are more efficient and reliable, and easier to keep clean. There are a couple of variations – the two-phase system and the three-phase system. A three-phase system has three exits, for oil, water and pomace. The two-phase has two exits, because it expels the water together with the pomace. The two-phase is said to produce a superior quality oil. This is because the three-phase system adds a significant quantity of water during the process, which washes out a portion of the polyphenols that play an important role in determining the flavour and stability of the oil. Unfortunately the two-phase is not as efficient at extracting a large quantity of oil.

Another, albeit less common, method is the 'Sinolea'. This works by vibrating stainless steel blades through the mash, bringing the oil to the surface where it can be skimmed off.

The Sinolea can produce an excellent quality oil; unfortunately the system is expensive, and often must be combined with the centrifuge method to maximize oil extraction.

The freshly extracted oil must be carefully stored to prevent oxidization. Modern producers normally store the oil in clean stainless steel containers at a temperature of 10-18°C (50-65°F).

What makes a superior olive oil?

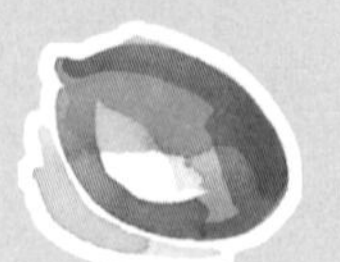

There are five main factors that influence the flavour and quality of an olive oil.

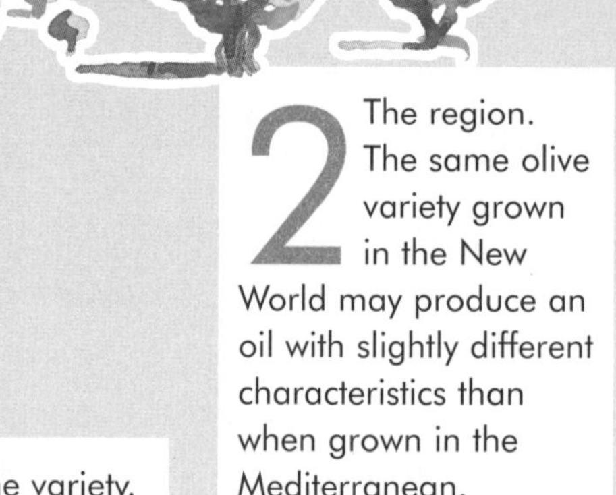

2 The region. The same olive variety grown in the New World may produce an oil with slightly different characteristics than when grown in the Mediterranean.

1 The variety. There are thousands of different olive varieties. Each has its own characteristics and there is no doubt that some produce a better quality of oil than others.

3 Maturity. This is one of the most important factors. An olive picked green will often produce a fresh, herbaceous or peppery oil. More mature fruit yields oil with more of a rounded, sweeter flavour.

4 Fruit health. Damaged fruit, or fruit that has not been milled quickly enough to prevent deterioration, can result in defective oil.

5 Good production and storage. Once picked, it is vital that the olives are processed rapidly and in a clean environment. Proper storage is also vital to preserve the delicate flavours of the oil.

Olive oil production and the environment

The milling process results in three products – the oil itself and waste products in the form of solid waste and a bitter substance called alpechin (also known as 'olive mill waste water'). The solid waste can be recycled as a heating fuel and for baking bricks and ceramics. However, alpechin – which is toxic and foul-smelling – has become a major environmental problem for the main olive oil-producing countries. Spain alone produces two million tonnes every year.

For years alpechin was simply discharged into rivers, but this is now banned by European Union (EU) legislation. Today most of the waste water is stored and left to evaporate in man-made pools. However, environmentalists contend that these pools have a negative impact on the regional environment, and there remains the risk of contamination to surface- and ground-water sources.

To tackle this problem, the EU has been funding a variety of projects with the aim of developing more environmentally sustainable solutions, in particular by promoting the use of technology to allow controlled biodegradation. There are already numerous methods used to treat alpechin, including filtration and chemical purification. Another

More producers are recognizing the need to develop more environmentally sustainable approaches to olive oil production

approach, which is already heavily used in Italy, is to spread the waste water on cultivated soil – a form of biological treatment. Regulation and controls are required in this case to prevent contamination of ground-water sources.

The pressure on the industry to deal with this problem is likely to increase as consumers become more aware of ecological issues, and as environmental regulations in general become tougher. Encouragingly, there are signs that more producers are recognizing the need to develop more environmentally sustainable approaches to olive oil production. In a 2004 survey of over 1,100 European olive oil businesses conducted by TDC OLIVE (an EU-funded project), 78 per cent of respondents said they would like to increase their general knowledge of environmental legislation, and 72 per cent wanted more information on systems of support and grants for the processing of waste.

Where in the world?

To most people, olive oil is inextricably linked with the Mediterranean. This is not surprising given all the publicity surrounding the 'Mediterranean Diet' and its reliance on olive oil. This view has also been perpetuated by the dominance of Spain, Italy and Greece when it comes to oil production.

Yet the global market is much more diverse than it at first seems, with olive oil now being produced all over the world: Japan, Argentina, Croatia, Uruguay, the United States and Australia to name just a few countries. Some have been producing oil for centuries; others are the new kids on the block, hoping to take on the might of Spain and Italy – if not in quantity, certainly in quality.

For the consumer, it means there is a huge range of oils from which to choose. The downside is that the vast quantity on offer can seem daunting.

The leader-board

Spain is the undisputed leader as the world's biggest producer of olive oil, accounting for around 40 per cent. There can be a slight variation from year to year, depending on the harvest, but generally the world order in olive oil is as follows:

- **Spain**
- **Italy**
- **Greece**
- **Tunisia**
- **Turkey**
- **Syria**
- **Morocco**
- **Portugal**

Matters are further complicated by the fact that, just because an oil is from a certain area, there is no guarantee the oil will have a certain taste. If you're after a robust, green, peppery style, for instance, then Tuscany would be your best bet but it is not assured – much is at the whim of the producer.

Here we take a look at how oil production varies around the world and we select some of the best examples from each country, from the large well-established producers to small boutiques, so you can find the most interesting and high-quality oils around.

Who produces the best?

Olive oils are such a huge source of pride in the countries that produce them that every nation will defend their oils with passion and fervour, declaring that theirs is, of course, the best. The jury is out – you can make huge generalizations about which country produces the finest but to do so would be unfair. Much is down to individual producers – even countries that are considered to be at the lower end of the olive oil market have producers who are making oils that buck the trend and wow the critics.

As a guide, look to respected competitions such as the Los Angeles International Extra Virgin Olive Oil Competition (formerly the LA County Fair Olive Oils of the World competition), L'Orciolo d'Oro and the International Olive Award.

AUSTRALIA

Australia's olive oil industry goes back to the 1800s and thrived for around a century before falling into decline, with factors including urban expansion and the high cost of labour compared to European countries leading to its downfall. However, interest started to re-awaken in the 1990s due to the increase in popularity of Mediterranean cuisine and the growing emphasis on healthier eating.

There are groves throughout Australia, and a number of cultivars are grown including the Tuscan varieties Frantoio, Correggiolo and Leccino, the Israeli Barnea and the Spanish Picual. Extensive planting is taking place and it is estimated that, by 2011, the country could be producing 40,000-50,000 tonnes of oil.

Dandaragan Estate

In the mid-1990s, a group of entrepreneurs decided the time was right to start a high-quality olive oil estate in Australia. After extensive research, they chose the Moore River region of Western Australia. Several varieties of olive trees have been planted including the Italian varieties Frantoio, Leccino, Correggiolo and Pendolino and the Spanish Manzanillo, Picual and Nevadillo Blanco. Unlike smaller, traditional European estates, Dandaragan uses the latest technology and harvesting methods such as training the trees to grow in a way that enables over-row harvesters to be used, adapted from the grape industry. Such machines help large groves to be harvested quickly at the optimum time. Its last harvest resulted in four blends: Delicate, Fruity, Robust and Chefs' Choice (sold directly to restaurants).

FRANCE

While olive oil may be integral to many French dishes, as a country France is a relatively small producer compared to other European olive-producing countries. In fact, the French consume much more than they produce, so the export market is tiny.

The olive oil industry in France was hit badly in 1956 by a big freeze which wiped out a large proportion of trees. Production now is small – in 2006-7, the country produced 4,700 tonnes compared to Italy's 630,000.

Alziari

This pale golden oil, which some argue is the best olive oil in France, has a sweet, delicate aroma, with herbaceous notes. Established in 1868, the mill is the oldest in Nice and traditional techniques are still used to produce the oil, which is made using the Cailletier or 'nicoise' olive.

Mill Jean-Marie Cornille

The Vallée des Baux is known for four main cultivars – Salonenque, Béruguette, Verdale and Grossane – and the producers around the region make prized oils. They include those from Mill Jean-Marie Cornille, which uses traditional granite mills to produce a very sweet, elegant oil that is golden-green in colour.

GREECE

Greece is home to some 140 million olive trees. It produces over 400,000 tonnes of olive oil a year, making it the third-biggest producer in the world. However, the Greeks are the biggest consumers of olive oil, using over 20 litres per person a year. The main production areas are centred on Crete and the Peloponnese.

Iliada

Although the bottle may say Kalamata, the oil is not made from Kalamata olives but Koroneiki olives grown in Kalamata. There are two oils available: the Iliada Extra Virgin Olive Oil is quite robust with a chilli kick to it, whereas the organic variety is lighter, more subtle and very versatile, with fruit and nut flavours.

Gaea

Gaea, meaning mother earth, was founded in 1995 to bring high-quality regional Greek produce to the international market. One of its award-winning products is its olive oil from Sitia in eastern Crete, which is made solely from cold-pressed Koroneiki olives. It is a fruity, well-balanced oil, with good herbaceous notes and a slight kick.

Bläuel

Bläuel was set up in 1980 by Austrian Fritz Bläuel who had moved to the Peloponnese around ten years earlier. Having seen much of the good-quality olive oil bound for Italy in big silos, he started to fill individual bottles by hand, winning the support of the villagers. The company instigated organic farming methods and, so far, 500 farms have become organic with more under way. Bläuel's Mani Organic Extra Virgin Olive Oil has won much acclaim, being fruity and slightly spicy.

ITALY

Tuscan olive oil is held in such esteem and enjoys so much of the spotlight you'd be forgiven for thinking that it is all Italy produces. This is far from the truth, as Tuscan oil is only a small part of the picture and is way behind the likes of Puglia and Calabria, the two main oil-producing regions, when it comes to quantity. Italy is second in importance to Spain in terms of production.

Seggiano

Made solely from the Olivastra olive variety, this rich, golden-green oil is more delicate than many other Tuscan oils yet is still rich and flavourful, with a slight sweetness. The Olivastra is unique to the village of Seggiano and a few neighbouring areas and, as it can withstand both high and low temperatures, it is ideally suited to the mountain climate – Seggiano sits on the slopes of Monte Amiata, an extinct volcano.

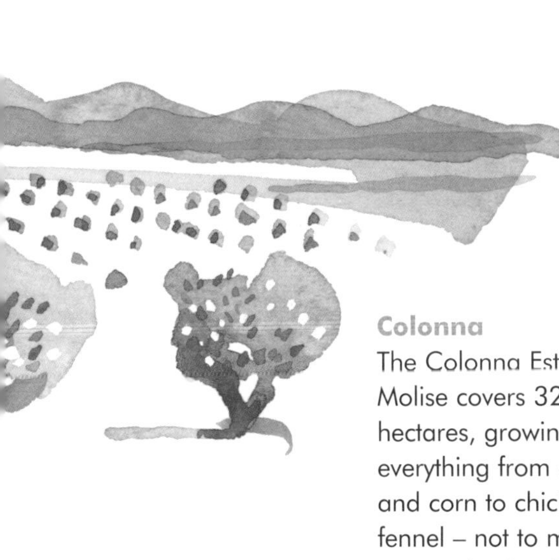

Barbera

This Sicilian-based producer is acclaimed for its excellent range of blended olive oils. The family-run business carefully selects and controls which olive groves it uses and the result is wonderful oils such as Stupor Mundi, which mixes both Sicilian (Biancolilla) and transplanted Apulian (Coratina) cultivars, producing a complex and fragrant oil. Other Barbera oils include the highly popular Frantoia, which is rich and green-gold, with a good peppery hit.

Colonna

The Colonna Estate in Molise covers 320 hectares, growing everything from cereals and corn to chickpeas and fennel – not to mention the crops raised to feed the 600 Comisana pedigree sheep which produce the estate's cheese and milk. Olive groves take up 70 hectares, and the farm uses a mixture of traditional techniques alongside the latest technology, with the harvest taking place before the olives are fully ripe, using pneumatic combs or vibrating equipment to shorten picking times. The estate's range includes the Molise, a blend of oils from varieties indigenous to the area, which has Protected Designation of Origin status: it's mild, herbaceous, with hints of apple and almond. Its Colonna Estate oil is highly regarded – it is grassy with notes of artichoke.

ITALY continued

Capezzana

Capezzana, near Florence, has long been a centre for olive and wine production – some records have dated it as far back as 1,200 years. The tradition is still continued but, under the aristocratic family of Contini Bonacossi, who now own the estate, production techniques have been modernized and the olives are processed in the estate's continuous cycle olive mill, which uses mild centrifugation on the crushed olive paste. Its oil is made mainly from Moraiolo and Frantoio olives as well as a small percentage of Pendolino and Leccino varieties, resulting in a well-balanced oil with a peppery bite that mellows into a fruity, warm aftertaste.

Disisa

This Sicilian producer has two excellent olive oils. The extra virgin olive oil is made from Cerasuola olives and has a clean, herbaceous taste, and the Tesoro Val di Mazara, which has Protected Denomination of Origin status. The latter is a blend of olives including Cerasuola, Nocellara del Belice and Biancolilla, giving it a complex, well-balanced flavour of fruit and pepper.

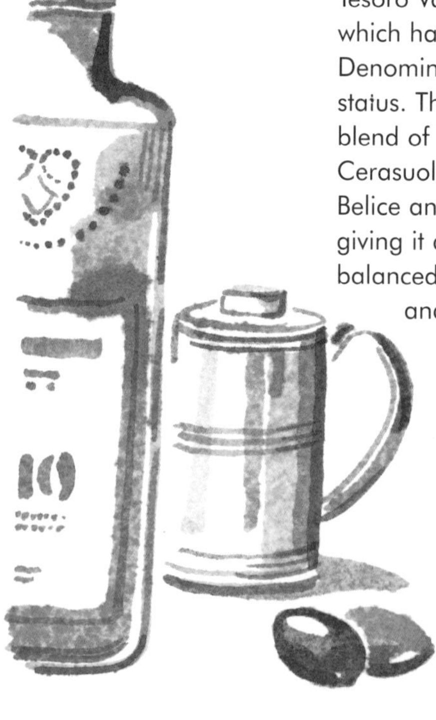

THE MIDDLE EAST

The tradition of oil production in the Middle East dates back thousands of years and it is still a highly valued commodity in the region. Syria, for example, is the world's fifth-biggest producer, with well over 65 million olive trees.

Jordan has around 17 million olive trees, with many more planted each year, and typical cultivars include Nabali, Rasie and Souri. Efforts are being made to increase efficiency and also to shorten the times between picking and processing.

JORDAN

Terra Rossa

The new emphasis on high technology is demonstrated by the likes of JomoFOOD. Its complex just outside Amman has a museum, a restaurant bringing together the olive traditions and cuisines of the Middle East and Mediterranean and, of course, a state-of-the-art oil mill. The company's plan is to target international markets with its wide range of products – and it has met with considerable success, winning several awards. Its premium olive oil is the Sinolea, followed by the EVOO (extra virgin olive oil). The Sinolea is extracted using a natural cold-drip method and is unfiltered, while the EVOO is extracted using a centrifugal cold-pressed method and is filtered. Both are organic, with the olives picked early in the harvest while they are still half green, intense, fresh and fruity.

NEW ZEALAND

Although New Zealand's oldest commercial plantings are only in their second decade, the country is producing some excellent oils. New Zealand has no indigenous olive trees and many 'local' trees are thought to have been propagated from olives brought into the country in the 19th century. Common local varieties include One Tree Hill, Tamaki and Motu – some were named after their geographical region or even the person who propagated them.

Commercial plantings have seen more of an emphasis on traditional Mediterranean varieties such as Frantoio and Picual. Exact production figures are hard to come by. However, figures for 2006 from the 400 members of the Olives New Zealand industry association record a harvest of 1,600 tonnes of olives, which produced approximately 190,000 litres of extra virgin olive oil. There is a strict assessment to qualify for ONZ Certification, which is based on the International Olive Council standards for extra virgin olive oil.

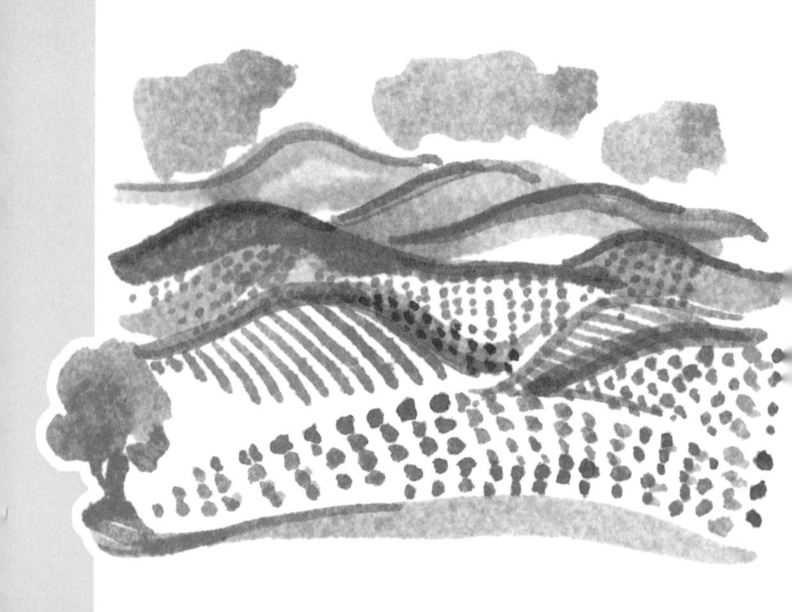

Rangihoua Estate

Rangihoua Estate only started developing olive groves in 1996 but it has since gone on to win awards around the world. The estate is on Waiheke Island, which is situated in the Hauraki Gulf off the coast of Auckland and has its own microclimate with a long, hot, dry summer, making it ideal for both olives and grapes. It produces a number of oils but its flagship is the Stonyridge Blend, which has notes of hay, apple and rosemary, with a light peppery finish.

Serendipity

On this estate, located in the Marlborough district at the top of the South Island, planting only began in 1997. Now 10,000 olive trees cover 32 hectares of what was once sheep pasture. A number of cultivars have been planted including Frantoio and Leccino from Italy, Barnea from Israel, and Picholine from France. Its oils are fruity, with notes of apple and cut grass.

NORTH AFRICA

The olive oil industry in North Africa has long been held back because of a lack of modern processing practices. Things are changing and investment is now being seen in some parts of the region.

In terms of production, there is much potential. Tunisia is the world's fourth-largest producer of olive oil and has over 58 million olive trees.

Morocco's olive oil industry is based on the Picholine Marocaine olive variety (accounting for 96 per cent) which is hardy and well suited to the country's soil and climate.

MOROCCO

Volubilia
Volubilia shows just how good Moroccan olive oil can be and its excellence has been recognized by the Italian Guide Extravergine 2006 in its annual awards. The oil, from the Meknès-Tafilalet region, is made from hand-picked olives that are pressed immediately with a modern temperature-controlled system.

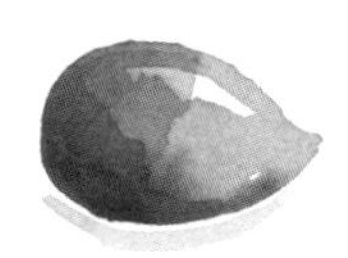
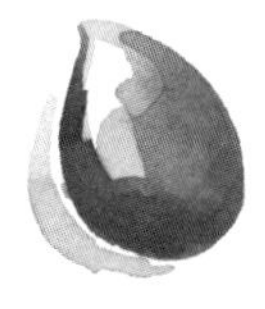
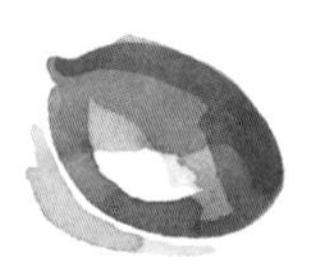

PORTUGAL

Portugal's olive industry is small compared to its European neighbours, producing 40,000 tonnes of oil per year compared to 400,000 in Greece. Portuguese oil has been known for tasting slightly rancid or oxidized, which fans say is a positive characteristic typical of the Portuguese style. However, things are changing and there are many producers now making oils in a more modern style.

CARM Praemium

CARM (Casa Agrícola Roboredo Madeira) is a family business that dates back to the 17th century. Located in the Douro Valley, the estate stretches around the village of Almendra, with 220 hectares of olive groves and 62 hectares of vineyards. The high temperatures and low rainfall on the stony-steep slopes have been utilized since the 8th century for cultivating vines, olives and almonds and they are now in the capable hands of this organic farm, which produces a number of highly regarded wines and oils. Among its oils is CARM Praemium, which has a bouquet of ripe tomato and apple, and a great balance of fruit and pepper.

Quinta Vale de Lobos

In the 1860s/1870s, Quinta Vale de Lobos (Valley of Wolves Estate) was the home of Portuguese writer Alexandre Herculano. He had a particular interest in farming, and his olive oil won much acclaim. Quinta Vale de Lobos' oil is still highly regarded and is blended from olives from both old and new groves planted on the estate. The varieties include Galega, Cobrançosa, Picual, Blanqueta and Arbequina, with the olives pressed within one to two hours of picking. It is fresh, appley, with hints of almonds and a slight pepper finish.

SOUTH AFRICA

Olives have been grown in South Africa since the 17th century – Jan van Riebeeck, the founder of Cape Town, apparently noted in his diary in 1661 that two olive trees were growing successfully on a Cape farm. But it wasn't until the early 1900s that olive oil became a commercial enterprise. The industry has grown slowly but surely since, mainly through the work of wine estates looking for alternative income sources when the wine harvest has ended.

Morgenster

Italian-born Giulio Bertrand bought the Morgenster estate in 1992 with no intention of producing olive oil. Yet the rolling hills reminded him so much of Tuscany, he set about establishing a vineyard and an olive grove. Cultivars were imported from Italy and grown on the slopes around Somerset West. The resulting oil, a blend of five different olive varieties, is continually winning awards around the world. It was judged the Best Blended Olive Oil in the world in the Italian competition L'extravergine, and was also the first South African olive oil to win one of Italy's L'Orciolo d'Oro awards, which it has now done seven years in a row. It is fresh and full-bodied, with a hint of pepper.

Willow Creek Estate

At the foot of the Langeberg mountains in the Western Cape, Willow Creek Estate has been farmed since 1793 but it wasn't until 2002 that it pressed its first oil. It now has 140 hectares of olive trees and aims to double this in the next two years, making it one of the biggest estate olive oil producers in the southern hemisphere. Its extra virgin olive oil is well regarded internationally, as is the estate's limited edition Directors' Reserve, a blend of the directors' favourites that season.

SOUTH AMERICA

Whilst South America is now making a big impression around the world with its wines, its olive oil industry is still in its infancy. Yet there is great promise, and the market in terms of Chilean exports to the US alone has grown rapidly in the last few years. In 2006, Chile produced around 2,000 tonnes of extra virgin olive oil for export and this is expected to grow to 13,000 tonnes by 2015.

CHILE

Olave

This organic, award-winning oil makes the most of Chile's ideal olive-growing climate to produce a fruity oil made from Frantoio, Coratina, Arbequina and Leccino olives.

ARGENTINA

Olium

Whilst Argentina is not an area you'd readily associate with olive oil, it has several producers making an impact on the international stage. They include Mario Geier, whose Olium extra virgin olive oil has won prizes worldwide. Located in the microclimate of the Valle de Traslasierra, Córdoba, the estate produces its oil predominantly from Arbequina olives, blended with others including Farga, Arauco and Nevadillo. It is a ripe, fruity, oil with notes of fresh herbs and bananas.

Spain is the leading exporter of oils, shipping to over 100 countries, including Italy, France, Portugal and the UK

SPAIN

Spain is the largest producer of olive oil in the world, with annual production averaging 700,000 to 800,000 tonnes a year. The country has a staggering 300 million olive trees covering over two million hectares, 92 per cent of which are dedicated to oil production. It is the leading exporter of oils, shipping to over 100 countries, including Italy, France, Portugal and the UK. Much of Spain's olive oil production is centred on Andalusia, but groves are found all over Spain, including the regions of Catalonia, Castilla la Mancha and Aragon.

Traditionally, Spanish olive oil is quite sweet, fruity and golden in colour, but big changes in production techniques and the introduction of more cultivars have led to a more varied, and more sophisticated, range of oils becoming available.

Núñez de Prado

This is one of the most highly regarded oils in the world. Baena, in the Cordoba province, is home to the Núñez de Prado family's olive estates, which have been producing premium oil since 1795. Only fruits which have turned from purple to black are picked, by hand, and at the end of each session the olives are sent to the mill to be processed immediately. The oil is what it calls Flor de Aceite, or the Flower of the Oil, consisting only of the oil that has dripped from the fruit naturally. The oil is organic, has hints of apples, oranges and almonds, and is packaged in individually numbered bottles with a label printed with an invitation to visit the mill.

Marques de Valdueza

Marques de Valdueza is credited with being a more modern, sophisticated Spanish oil than you might ordinarily expect. Using a blend of Arbequina, Picual, Hojiblanca and Morisca olives grown on the Perales de Miraflores estate in Extremadura in the west of Spain, this extra virgin oil has a fresh and fruity taste with a bouquet of fresh grass and apples. Its excellence has been recognized by the International Olive Oil Council, which awarded it a score of 8.5 out of 9.

Lérida Extra Virgin Olive Oil

The Spanish province of Lleida, or Lérida, is ideal for growing the Arbequina tree, and the family-run estate of the Veá family makes good use of the conditions to produce a fruity, green oil, with traces of apple and complex nutty overtones. Only small, lean Arbequina olives are used to make the oil, and they are harvested early while slightly under-ripe. The cultivation process is organic, and olives are picked by hand.

Aguibal

Aguibal is the label under which you can find fine, single varietal olive oils: Picual, Arbequina and Manzanilla. Its Manzanilla is known for its robust, complex, rich flavours; the creamy Arbequina – unusual as it is an Andalusian Arbequina rather than from northern Spain – has hints of almond and fresh tomato; while its Picual is light and herbal.

THE UNITED STATES

Currently the US consumes around 200 million litres of olive oil (7 per cent of the world's olive oil) a year. This is far more than it actually produces. US olive oil production is centred on California, which makes just 360,000 litres each year. Demand for premium oils is increasing exponentially (in 2006 it was reported that US domestic sales had gone up 20 per cent each year for the previous five years).

The olive was brought to California in the 18th century by Spanish missionaries and for a while the industry thrived before falling into decline. Now, however, olive oil is enjoying a huge renaissance, with consumers choosing it for its appeal as a gourmet product as well as its health benefits. Many boutique producers have opened up and there has been a trend to plant Italian cultivars in order to imitate the high-quality Tuscan oils.

The California Olive Oil Council was set up in 1992 to promote the burgeoning industry, and it runs a quality-control programme. To qualify, producers must demonstrate that their oils meet certain requirements including:

- The oil is mechanically extracted without chemicals or excessive heat.
- The oil has an acidity level, in terms of oleic free fatty acid, of not more than 0.5 per cent.
- Positive taste elements and no taste defects, as determined during a blind tasting.

Lila Jaeger

One of the founding members of the Californian Olive Oil Council, Lila Jaeger helped to pioneer the growth of the olive industry in the Napa Valley in the 1990s. She discovered the potential of the old olive trees on her estate, which were later supplemented with varietals from Europe. Today's award-winning oil is a blend of Aglandau, Bouteillan, Leccino, Farga and Cayon, and her family carry on the tradition of pressing the olives at the press in Glen Ellen, which is part of a co-operative of other regional oil makers. The flavour is at first sweet and grassy, which gives way to pepper, then finishes again on a sweet note.

California Olive Ranch

With a 280-hectare estate, California Olive Ranch is the largest and one of the most prolific olive oil producers in the country. COR imported a farming technique from Spain called High Density Plantings (HDPs), which allowed the estate to plant 1,656 semi-dwarf olive trees per hectare, versus the usual 296. Additionally, the semi-dwarf trees produce their first fruit after only two years, less than half the time of a typical olive oil tree. Its range includes the Arbequina, with notes of ripe tropical fruits; Estate Reserve Blend, made from Arbequina, Arbosana and Koroneiki, with a herbaceous flavour and hints of banana; and an oil known as Olio Nuovo, new oil bottled directly from the press with particles of olive flesh left in the product, meaning it has to be used within two to three months.

Choosing the right oil

There are thousands of olive oils to choose from, so where do you start and how do you make the most of your oil once you've bought it?

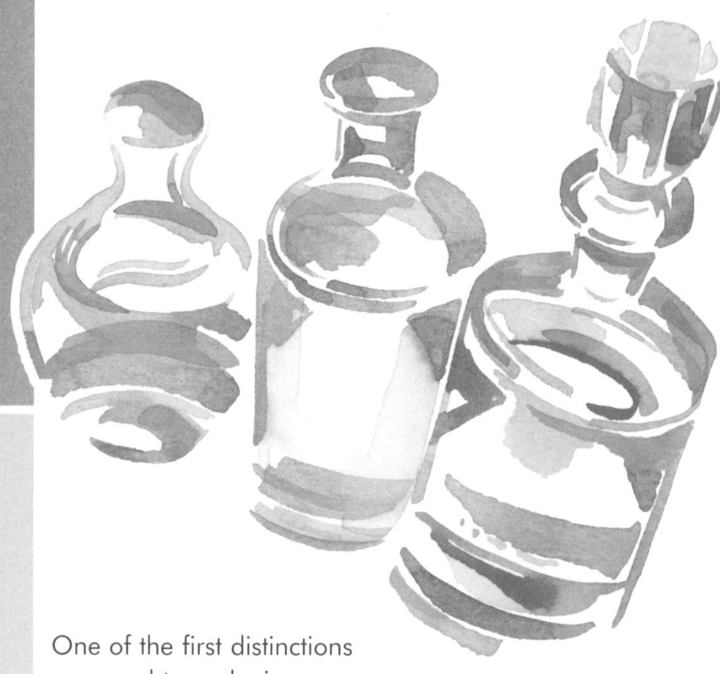

One of the first distinctions you need to make is between the different grades of olive oil. There are three that you will come across most often: extra virgin olive oil is the king of the olive oils – the premium grade oil. It has a lower acidity level than other grades and has other characteristics in taste, colour and aroma that make it a superior product. Virgin olive oil is the next grade down and will have a slightly higher acidity level.

Anything labelled 'olive oil' is a blend of virgin olive oil and olive oil that has been processed to make it fit for consumption – there are no rules on how much virgin oil goes into the final product.

You also need to consider what you want to use the oil for. Heating the oils can cause them to lose some of their flavour so, as extra virgin olive oil is more expensive, it is often recommended that people save this for drizzling on to foods raw or as a final addition to a dish. Spanish oils naturally go well with Spanish dishes, Tuscan oils with hearty bean soups and meat-based pasta dishes, and milder French oils with fish dishes.

Extra virgin olive oil has a lower acidity level than other grades and has other characteristics in taste, colour and aroma

But these are only rules of thumb and are as sweeping as saying that white wine is the only wine which should accompany fish. Much of it is down to personal preference and, to find yours, you'll need to learn how to taste the oils.

Tasting
Olive oil experts are skilled in discerning the many different characteristics of olive oil. They learn to evaluate its aroma and texture, and can identify the various subtleties of flavour.

There are often strict guidelines – such as only tasting mid-morning when the palate is at its most alert and making sure the oil is at a certain temperature. Fortunately for the consumer, it is much simpler than all that and all you have to decide is whether you like it or not.

However, if you do want to learn how to appreciate the different varieties of oil on offer, it helps to have some of the vocabulary. Tasting wheels have been developed such as that from olive oil expert Richard Gawel. It lists some 72 olive oil descriptors: for example, 'Fruity' is subdivided into

characteristics such as 'Lime' or 'Guava', and 'Fragrant' could include 'Floral' or 'Perfumed'. Defects can fall into categories such as 'Winey' or 'Muddy'. You can find the wheel online at www.aromadictionary.com/oliveoilwheel.html

The oils should be tasted in sequence, with the mildest first. Experts say the oil should be tasted on its own, direct from the glass, as even bread can change how the oil tastes. However, for first-time testers, the idea of taking a glug of olive oil can be off-putting. If that's the case, you can transfer the oil from the glass to a dish after smelling, then dip in small pieces of plain, seedless bread. Ideally, you should only drink water or eat slices of green apples as a palate cleanser. Your stomach should be empty, as that is when you're most receptive to all the different flavours.

OIL SELECTION

Pour about a tablespoon of oil into a glass and warm it slightly in your hands. First look at the colour. Although it is not an indication of quality, you might prefer one colour to another for aesthetic reasons. A dark green oil, for example, looks wonderful drizzled over feta cheese but not so appetizing over a piece of white fish – for that you'd want a light honey-coloured oil.

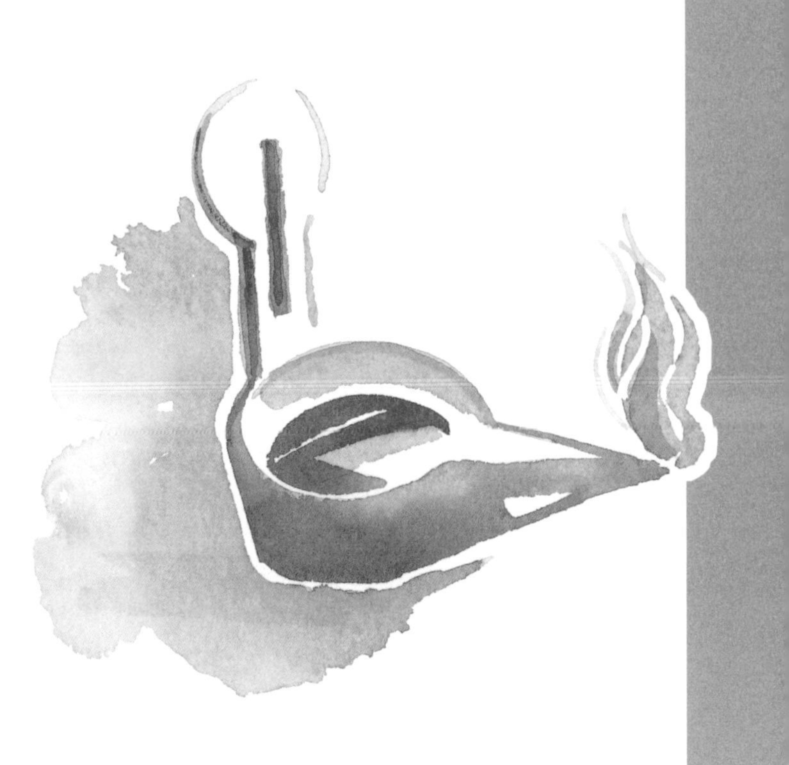

Then smell the oil. Take three short, deep sniffs, raising your nose away from the glass between each sniff. It is now that it will become most obvious if the oil is off. Good oils should smell of the fruit. Then take a sip, drawing in a little air at the same time, and roll it around your mouth and over the tongue for about five seconds. Consider its texture on your tongue. You can then spit out some of it, but some should be swallowed to appreciate the bitterness or peppery qualities of the oil. You may find it catches in the throat – this slight burn is highly desirable in an olive oil. It's worth noting that, if you find an oil too peppery, you could see what happens when the bottle has been opened for a few weeks and allowed to mellow.

You should always try to taste an oil before adding it to your cooking. Like wine, if it doesn't taste good in the glass, don't cook with it. It won't do anything to enhance your dish and could even make it taste unpleasant.

Buying

Most people will buy their olive oil from a supermarket. However, a specialist retailer should be able to offer specific advice on choosing an oil, taking into account your preferences and what you want to use the oil for. Additionally, they may have built up a good relationship with the producer, stocking only the new season's oils so you're not buying anything that has been sitting on a shelf for a while.

Age is one of the most important factors when choosing which oil to buy. Unlike wine, olive oil doesn't get better with age and only has a finite shelf-life. Look on the bottle for the harvest date. Some labels won't tell you this, but a good retailer should be able to. Unopened oils should last for around 12 to 18 months from the date of harvest. There's no hard and fast rule, however, as some varieties last longer than others. Again, a good retailer will be able to advise.

'Best before' or 'best by' dates may not always be a good indication of the freshness of the oil and there are different regulations around the world on what date actually appears on the bottle.

Always choose a retailer that has a high turnover of stock – they are more likely to have the freshest oils and there's less chance that the oil has been sitting around under a bright light for too long. Olive oil is particularly sensitive to light so only buy oils in dark glass or opaque containers. Plastic isn't too great for oil either as oil can take on the properties of the container.

Only buy as much as you can use in a month. It may seem less economical, but it is far better than having to tip the oil away because it has gone rancid. If you want to buy that big bottle, consider sharing it between friends, transferring it into smaller dark glass bottles.

Reading the labels
There can be quite a bit of jargon on olive oil labels and, to make matters even more complex, there is no one international standard. However, there are a few terms you can keep an eye out for to help distinguish the facts from the marketing hype.

Acidity Good quality oil has a low acidity – but don't assume that it is a case of the lower the better.

Filtered, non-filtered
Most oils are now filtered to remove any sediment. However, some connoisseurs actually prefer oils that retain some of the sediment and believe they have more flavour. Unfiltered oils will need to be used up more quickly than filtered.

Estate Oils/Single Estate Oils/Estate Grown Oils are produced with olives from one site, and pressed and bottled on that site. They're often expensive but high in quality.

Know your oils

The International Olive Council classifies olive oil as follows:

'Virgin olive oils are the oils obtained from the fruit of the olive tree solely by mechanical or other physical means under conditions, particularly thermal conditions, that do not lead to alterations in the oil, and which have not undergone any treatment other than washing, decantation, centrifugation and filtration.'

Hand-picked The implication is that inferior olives would have been discarded so that only the high-quality olives were pressed.

Imported from This doesn't mean that all the oil in this product is from that particular country, and it may contain oils from several sources.

Pure olive oil The name implies that there is something superior about the oil. However, all it means is that it contains no other kind of oil and is a blend of virgin olive oil and refined (processed) olive oil.

First pressing This is pretty much a redundant term now as production methods have changed so there is usually no second pressing.

Cold-pressed Producers must ensure that temperatures during processing do not exceed 27°C (80°F).

Blended Many major olive oil manufacturers will blend their oils, as crops may taste different each year. By blending from a number of sources, they can ensure their products have a consistent taste.

PDO Protected Denomination of Origin guarantees that the oil is produced in a certain area and that it has the typical characteristics of that area.

Extra virgin olive oil Virgin olive oil which has a free acidity, expressed as oleic acid, of not more than 0.8g per 100g.

Virgin olive oil Virgin olive oil which has a free acidity, expressed as oleic acid, of not more than 2g per 100g.

Olive oil A blend of refined olive oil and virgin olive oils. It has a free acidity, expressed as oleic acid, of not more than 1g per 100g.

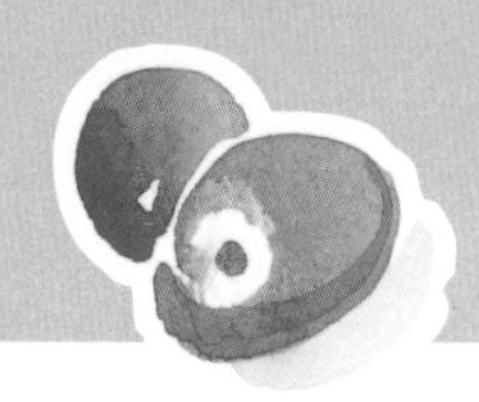

Storing

When you get your olive oil home, how you store it is crucial if you are to enjoy it at its peak. Oil does not like light or heat – they cause it to deteriorate quickly and turn rancid. A cool, dark cupboard is an ideal place to store your oil. Or if you have a wine cellar, store it in there and keep a little in the kitchen for everyday use. Cupboards situated right next to your oven are to be avoided. Always close the container tightly after use.

Rancidity in itself isn't harmful – indeed, some people actually prefer the taste. However, it really won't do that much for your Greek salad, and most people's palates would choose a peppy, fruity oil in preference to one that tastes off. If it tastes buttery it is likely to be rancid.

Olive oil can be refrigerated to keep it as fresh as possible. It might turn cloudy and solidify in the fridge but bringing it back to room temperature should see the oil turn clear again.

There are many deliciously flavoured oils you can make at home, by infusing them with herbs, for example. However, they should be stored in the fridge and used within a few days as bacteria can build up in the oil, which may cause botulism. Dried herbs and spices are a much safer option, and the flavoured oil can be kept longer.

Cooking

Olive oil can lose some of its flavour when heated, so you are better off using the less expensive varieties for cooking. Save the more expensive extra virgin oils for salad dressings or add a glug or two to your dish before serving.

Simple olive oil has much less flavour but, because of the refining process, it is good for cooking at high temperatures.

Olive oils labelled as 'mild' or 'light' have a very subtle flavour so can be used as a substitute for butter and other fats when making desserts or more delicately flavoured dishes. Mild-flavoured oils are also ideal for baking, and produce moister cakes. You'll also need less olive oil than butter when baking. Say, for example, one teaspoon butter/ margarine is called for in a recipe, you only need three-quarters of a teaspoon of olive oil.

Olive oil can also be used alongside butter – a little olive oil can help stop the butter from burning when you are frying.

As olive oil doesn't degrade as quickly as other oils, it can stand repeated high heating and you can use the oil around three times, if you're not using it for particularly strong flavours and you filter it each time.

Store cupboard essentials
Olive oil enthusiasts often have a wide variety of oils stashed away in their cupboard, each one serving a different purpose. However, given olive oil is best used as quickly as possible, having just a few oils on the go at any one time might be best. Three to four small bottles of olive oil of different types will provide you with all the versatility you will need at first.

Extra virgin olive oil
Choose a deep green, peppery style. You want a robust oil that will make highly flavoured dressings, marinades and a dip for bread. Try it drizzled over a hearty Tuscan-style soup.

Virgin olive oil
Choose a light gold, milder, less peppery oil. This will be ideal for lighter salad dressings where you don't want such a distinctive oil flavour. Use it to drizzle over fish or over a warmed dish of cannellini beans and basil.

Olive oil Choose a mild-tasting, honey-coloured olive oil. This is your everyday oil to be used for cooking.

Light olive oil A lightly flavoured oil is ideal for baking or frying where you don't want an overwhelming flavour.

Recipes

Having tasted some of the many olive oils on offer, you probably know which ones you prefer and how you like to use them. For the recipes in this chapter, we have only suggested a particular variety if we feel strongly that you need a certain style of oil. Otherwise, we leave it to your discretion, keeping in mind that, if you're not cooking with the oil, use the best quality extra virgin olive oil you can find.

We've also assumed that you will have to hand some black pepper in a grinder for seasoning. We also recommend coarse sea salt in a number of recipes. We find Maldon salt from the UK to be the best as it has the perfect-sized crystals to add the right amount of both crunch and flavour to the dish. The French fleur de sel is also excellent.

STARTERS AND LIGHT DISHES

Chilli Roasted Almonds

A great nibble for a dinner party – easy to make and certainly beats the usual dish of potato chips.

- A generous glug of olive oil (about 125 ml/4 fl oz/½ cup) for frying
- A bag of raw, blanched almonds (you can vary the amounts depending on how many people you are serving)
- Chilli pepper flakes
- Coarse sea salt

Heat the oil in a large frying pan. Add the almonds and toss them in the oil. Allow them to turn colour slightly, then add the chilli pepper flakes and salt to taste. If you don't like the almonds to taste too spicy, this recipe works just as well if the chilli flakes are replaced with rosemary.

Bruschetta

A great starter to make when the barbecue is being fired up as it will toast the bread perfectly. Use the ripest, reddest tomatoes you can find.

Serves 4

- 6 tomatoes
- A good handful of fresh basil (about 120 g/4 oz/½ cup), shredded
- 6 tbsp olive oil
- 2 tsp balsamic vinegar
- Sea salt and black pepper
- 1 ciabatta, cut into slices 1 cm/½ in thick
- 3 garlic cloves

Chop the tomatoes into a rough dice, then mix in a bowl with the basil, oil and vinegar. Season well. Heat a griddle or a barbecue, then toast the bread on both sides until golden and the slices have coloured with the black bars of the barbecue. Rub the garlic over the surface of the bread, then top with the tomatoes.

Crostini

Crostini make canapés very easy to do and they are so much more appealing than a soggy vol-au-vent.

For the toast

- 1 baguette
- Olive oil

Preheat the oven to 200°C/400°F/gas mark 6. Fill a saucer with olive oil. Cut the baguette into rounds about 1 cm/ ½ in thick and dip (not drench) each side into the oil. You'll need to keep topping the saucer up with oil. Place the rounds on a rack over a baking tray and cook for 10 minutes or until the bread is nicely toasted. Leave them to cool. Make them around an hour before you want to serve but not much more so they retain their crunch.

For the toppings

A wide variety of toppings can be made – but around three is enough for a small drinks party.

Goat's cheese and tapenade

Spread each crostini with black olive tapenade and crown with 1 tsp of soft goat's cheese.

Green pea and mint

Cook 150 g/5 oz frozen peas in boiling water. Drain and tip into a food processor with 1 tbsp chopped mint and 1 tbsp extra virgin olive oil. Process to a smooth paste. Season and spread over the crostini. Top with shavings of parmesan.

Green olive

In a food processor, combine 225 g/8 oz stoned (pitted) green olives with 1 tbsp capers, 2 garlic cloves and 1 tbsp of olive oil.

Smoked salmon and cream cheese

Spread the cheese over the crostini, top with slivers of salmon and a sprinkling of dill. Drizzle with a little lemon juice and olive oil.

Gazpacho

A chilled soup for a hot summer's day. Use your best Spanish oil for drizzling and serve with a cold glass of dry sherry.

Serves 4

- 1 tbsp cumin seeds
- 2 garlic cloves
- 6 large tomatoes, skinned
- 450 ml/16 fl oz/2 cups tomato juice
- 2 red onions
- 2 sticks celery
- 4 tbsp olive oil
- 2 tbsp red wine vinegar
- ½ large or 1 small cucumber, peeled, seeded and diced
- 1 red bell pepper, seeded, ribs removed, cut into small dice

---

Crush the cumin and garlic in a mortar with a pestle. Put the tomatoes and juice, onions, celery, oil, vinegar, plus the cumin and garlic/cumin paste into a blender and blend until smooth. Add a little cold water until the liquid is the consistency of a thick soup. Season well, and refrigerate until ready to serve. Then add the diced cucumber and pepper. Serve in bowls with a drizzle of good Spanish olive oil.

Green Summer Vegetables with Pancetta

For a vegetarian version, or equally if you want a lighter dish, omit the pancetta and mix 2 tbsp of olive oil with 1 tbsp of lemon juice, using it to coat the cooked vegetables.

Serves 4

- 3 tbsp olive oil
- 200 g/7 oz pancetta (pork belly), diced
- 500 g/1 lb 2 oz/4 cups fresh green mixed vegetables (broad beans, sugar snap peas, garden peas)
- Coarse salt and freshly ground black pepper

Heat 1 tbsp of the oil in a pan and fry the pancetta until crisp. Remove from the pan and drain on kitchen paper. Cook the vegetables in boiling water until tender but still slightly crisp – not more than 2 to 3 minutes. Drain off the water and return the vegetables to the pan along with the pancetta and the rest of the olive oil, just to warm them through, stirring occasionally. Season well before serving.

Pasta Pomodoro

The secret of this simple tomato sauce is in the olive oil. Use plenty and drizzle over the finished dish.

Serves 2

- 2 tbsp olive oil for frying, plus peppery extra-virgin olive oil for drizzling
- 1 onion, finely chopped
- 1 garlic clove, finely chopped
- 1 x 400 g/14 oz can good-quality chopped tomatoes
- 1 glass (125 ml/4 fl oz/½ cup) wine (white or red) or water
- 2 tsp dried oregano
- 1 tsp dried chilli pepper flakes (optional)
- Dried pasta for two, preferably penne (about 250 g/8 oz)
- Handful of fresh basil, shredded
- Freshly grated parmesan or Pecorino cheese, to serve

Add the olive oil to a saucepan and, on a low heat, fry the onion and garlic until softened, taking care not to let them colour. Add the tomatoes, wine or water, oregano, and chilli pepper flakes, if using. Bring to the boil, then simmer for 30 minutes or until the sauce is thick and sweet. Add a little water and reduce the heat further if it looks like the sauce is drying out. Meanwhile, cook the pasta in plenty of salted, boiling water and drain it. Season the tomato sauce well. Stir in the pasta, add the basil and serve with the cheese sprinkled on top. Put the bottle of olive oil on the table to be used as a condiment.

Pasta with Aubergine (eggplant)

Serves 4

- 2 aubergines (eggplant)
- olive oil for frying
- 1 garlic clove, finely chopped
- 1 tsp dried chilli powder
- 1 x 400 g/14 oz can chopped tomatoes
- 3 tbsp pitted black olives
- Handful of fresh basil, shredded
- Dried pasta for four (large shells are good for this recipe)
- Pecorino cheese to serve

Cut the aubergines (eggplant) into 1 cm/½ in cubes. Place in a colander and sprinkle with salt. Leave for 30 minutes to remove the excess moisture. Rinse and pat dry. Heat a good glug of olive oil in a large pan and fry the aubergines (eggplant) until golden. Add the garlic and chilli. Add the chopped tomatoes, then simmer until the sauce thickens slightly. Meanwhile, cook the pasta in plenty of salted, boiling water. Add the olives to the pasta sauce and heat through. Stir in the basil. Drain the pasta and stir into the sauce. Serve with grated Pecorino cheese.

Humous

A delicious dip for summer parties. Serve with sticks of raw carrots, celery and cucumber.

- 400 g/14 oz can chick-peas, drained and rinsed
- 2 garlic cloves, peeled
- Juice of a lemon
- 2 tbsp tahini
- 3 tbsp olive oil
- Salt and freshly ground black pepper
- To serve: extra virgin olive oil
- 3 tbsp pine kernels, lightly toasted

Blend the ingredients, except the pine kernels, until you have a smooth paste, adding a little water if the mixture is not liquid enough. It should be the consistency of thick cream. Season well, transfer to a serving dish and chill. Finish with a drizzle of extra virgin olive oil and sprinkle with the pine kernels before serving.

Spaghetti alla Puttanesca

Serves 4

- 4 tbsp extra-virgin olive oil, plus a drizzle for the spaghetti
- 2 fresh red chilli peppers, seeded and chopped
- 3 cloves garlic, finely chopped
- 110 g/4 oz/ ½ cup salt anchovies, drained
- 110 g/4 oz/ ½ cup pitted black olives, chopped
- 2 tbsp capers, drained
- 900 g/2 lb/4 cups tomatoes, skinned and chopped
- 2 tbsp tomato purée (paste)
- Dried spaghetti, enough for four (about 750 g/1 lb 4oz)
- Handful of chopped fresh basil (about 120 g/4 oz/½ cup)
- Freshly grated parmesan

Heat the olive oil in a saucepan over a medium-hot hob. Add the chilli peppers and garlic and stir for a minute or two until the garlic softens a little. Add the anchovies, olives, capers, tomatoes and tomato purée (paste). Reduce the heat to low and simmer the sauce, uncovered, for around 45 minutes, or until it thickens and reduces. Meanwhile, cook the spaghetti in plenty of salted, boiling water. Drain and toss with a little olive oil. Divide the spaghetti into four warmed pasta bowls, pour the sauce over it, and add the chopped basil and parmesan to finish.

Tabbouleh

This zingy Middle Eastern salad is ideal with barbecued chicken or served with a range of dips as a starter to be scooped up with hot pitta bread. Serves four as a side salad.

- 110 g/4 oz bulgur wheat
- 50 g/2 oz mint
- 50 g/2 oz flat-leaved parsley
- 4 spring onions (scallions)
- 3 ripe tomatoes
- 3 tbsp lemon juice
- 4 tbsp olive oil
- 2 tbsp lightly toasted hazelnuts, chopped (optional)

Soak the bulgur wheat in cold water for 20 minutes or until the grains have softened slightly. Chop the mint and parsley finely, dice the spring onions and tomatoes and add to a large serving bowl. Drain the wheat thoroughly, removing excess moisture with a clean kitchen towel. Tip the wheat into the bowl, add the lemon juice and olive oil and stir thoroughly. Add the hazelnuts, if using. Season generously and set aside for half an hour before serving, to give the flavours a chance to combine.

Tapenade

An olive fan's idea of heaven, this spread combines the fruit and the oil. Try it on lightly toasted French bread with a scoop of goat's cheese on top.

- 225 g/8 oz stoned (pitted) black olives
- 6 anchovies in oil, drained
- 2 tbsp capers
- 1 garlic clove, chopped
- 3-4 basil leaves
- 2 tbsp lemon juice
- 2 tbsp olive oil

Place all the ingredients in the bowl of a food processor, except for the olive oil. Blend, adding the oil slowly until a smooth paste is achieved. Transfer to a serving bowl and serve with crudités (raw dipping vegetables).

Olive Oil Mash

The addition of olive oil instead of butter makes a healthier, although no less calorific, dish. The more robust flavour goes well with dishes such as lamb shanks braised in red wine with rosemary.

- 4 medium potatoes, peeled and cut into chunks
- 5-6 tbsp olive oil
- Salt and freshly ground black pepper

Put the potatoes in a large pan and cover with water. Bring to the boil, then simmer for 15 to 20 minutes until tender, then drain. Return to the heat briefly and add the oil. Cook until the oil has warmed slightly, then mash the potatoes until fluffy. Season well.

Morcilla Breakfast Baguette

This isn't exactly an authentic recipe. However, the morcilla (blood sausage) brings a touch of Spain to your weekend brunch. You can substitute any kind of blood sausage, from the English black pudding to the French boudin noir.

Serves 2

- About 120 g/4 oz morcilla (blood sausage)
- 4 slices lean bacon
- 1 tomato, halved
- Olive oil for frying
- 2 tbsp extra virgin olive oil
- 2 large hunks of crusty baguette, split horizontally
- Strong mustard, preferably English

Fry the morcilla, bacon and tomato until the tomato is soft, the morcilla is cooked through and the bacon is crispy. Pour 1 tbsp olive oil over the bottom slice of each piece of baguette, mash the tomato over the top, add the morcilla and bacon, then top with a little mustard before adding the top half of the baguette.

Tuscan Bean Soup

A hearty winter soup. Choose your finest, most peppery green olive oil to drizzle over the finished soup and serve with warm, crusty ciabatta.

Serves 4-6

- About 125 ml/4 fl oz/½ cup olive oil
- 120 g/4 oz pancetta, cubed
- 1 onion, chopped
- 1 carrot, chopped
- 1 stick celery, chopped
- 2 cloves garlic, chopped
- 1 x 400 g/14 oz can tomatoes
- Red wine, water or chicken stock to cover
- A good handful of small dried pasta (such as penne)
- 2 bay leaves
- A handful of fresh chopped herbs (basil or parsley)

In a large, heavy-bottomed pan, heat the oil over medium heat then gently fry the pancetta, onion, carrot, celery and garlic. Pour in the tomatoes, stir, then fill the pan to about 2.5 cm/1 in from the top with either wine, water or chicken stock. Add the pasta and bay leaves and stir well. Bring to the boil then reduce the heat, cover and simmer for around 40 minutes. Stir occasionally. Keep an eye on the liquid levels and top up when necessary – you don't want the soup to boil down too far, but it needs to reduce enough so it is thick, rich and flavourful. Finish by sprinkling with the chopped herbs.

Spaghetti Carbonara

A classic, comforting Italian dish.

Serves 2

- 150 g/5 oz pancetta (pork belly), cubed
- 2 tbsp olive oil
- 4 egg yolks
- 150 ml/¹/₄ pint/²/₃ cup double (heavy) cream
- 4 tbsp parmesan, grated, plus extra to serve
- Dried spaghetti, enough for two (about 225 g/8 oz)
- Handful of basil (about 120 g/4 oz, chopped [optional])
- Salt and freshly ground pepper

In a saucepan, fry the pancetta in the olive oil until lightly crisped, taking care not to burn it. Beat together the eggs and cream in a bowl and season with a little salt and freshly ground pepper. Add the cheese. Cook the spaghetti, drain and return to the pan. Then stir in the pancetta, any remaining oil from the pan, and the eggs and cream. Stir well, add the basil if using, and grate with some extra parmesan to serve.

Huevos Rancheros

This 'ranch-style eggs' dish is a breakfast classic. Use a mild-flavoured olive oil.

Serves 4

For the sauce

- 3 tbsp olive oil
- 1 onion, chopped
- 1 sweet red (bell) pepper, chopped
- 1 sweet green (bell) pepper, chopped
- 1 tsp ground cumin
- 1/4 tsp cayenne pepper
- 1 tsp seeded and chopped jalapeño pepper, finely chopped
- 1 garlic clove, finely chopped
- 1 x 400 g/14 oz can tomatoes
- 3 tbsp chopped fresh coriander (cilantro)

To serve

- 4 corn tortillas
- 4 eggs
- Monterey Jack cheese, grated

In a saucepan, heat 2 tbsp of the oil, and gently fry the onions and peppers. Add the cumin, cayenne, jalapeño, and garlic, and stir. Add the tomatoes and simmer the mixture, uncovered, for 15 minutes or until reduced by one third. Season to taste, and stir in the coriander. Reserve and keep warm. Warm the tortillas. Heat the rest of the oil in a frying pan and fry the eggs. Arrange the tortillas on four warmed serving plates, top with the sauce and the fried egg and sprinkle with the cheese.

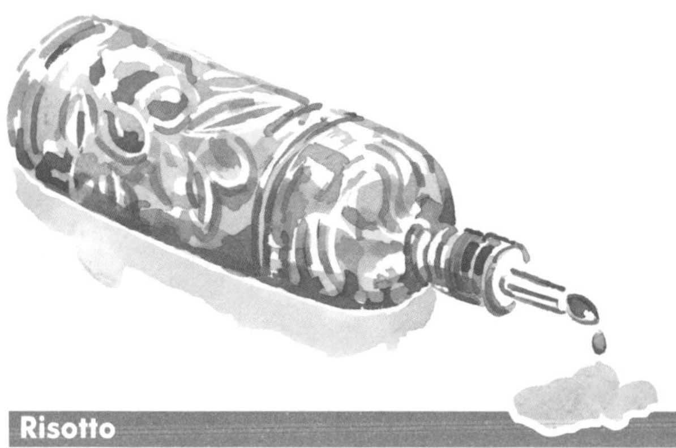

Risotto

A very simple dish but one that requires patience from the cook as the secret is in the long stirring and the slow addition of the stock. You can add a handful of lightly fried mushrooms – just stir them in before you add the parmesan.

Serves 4

- About 1.2 litres/2 pints/10 cups chicken stock (broth)
- 50 g/2 oz/¼ stick butter plus another 25 g/1 oz/ 2 tbsp butter to finish
- 2 tbsp olive oil
- 4 shallots, finely chopped
- ½ a stick celery, finely chopped
- 2 garlic cloves, finely chopped
- 400 g/14 oz/1½ cups short-grained (Italian) rice
- About 120 g/4 oz/1 cup grated parmesan cheese
- Coarse salt and freshly ground black pepper

Heat the stock and keep it simmering gently. In a heavy-bottomed pan, heat the butter and the oil and gently fry the shallots, celery and garlic, and gently soften, making sure it doesn't burn. Stir in the rice until it is well coated in the oil and butter. Keeping the rice on a moderate to high heat, pour a ladleful of the stock into the rice and stir until it is absorbed. Repeat with another ladleful and continue until the rice is just cooked. It should be soft but still slightly firm to the bite. You may not need all of the stock or you may need to add a little hot water. Remove the pan from the heat. Stir in the parmesan and butter. Season well with coarse salt and freshly ground black pepper. Cover with a lid and let the risotto stand for a minute or so until the cheese has melted a little. Serve immediately.

Herb and Olive Focaccia

- 500 g/1 lb 2oz strong plain (all-purpose) flour
- 1 tbsp salt
- 4 tbsp olive oil
- 25 g/1 oz fresh yeast or 1 package dry yeast
- 275 ml/10 fl oz/1 1/2 cups water
- 1 tbsp chopped fresh thyme leaves
- 2 tbsp chopped black olives

Put the flour, salt, olive oil, yeast, water and thyme into a large bowl and, using your hands, mix the ingredients together until you have a ball of dough. Lightly flour the work surface and knead the dough for five minutes. Place the dough back in the bowl, cover with a clean kitchen towel and leave for a couple of hours. Knead again, incorporate the olives into the dough and flatten into a circle. Leave for an hour. Oil a baking sheet, drizzle a little more oil over the top of the dough and bake at 230°C/450°F/gas mark 8 for 20 to 30 minutes.

Gambas Pil Pil

Spanish cooking really shows off what good olive oil can do for a dish. Try this tapa recipe – perfect for a drinks party.

Serves 4

- 150 ml/5 fl oz/2/3 cup olive oil
- 2 garlic cloves, sliced into slivers
- 2 tsp dried chilli pepper flakes
- 20 uncooked medium-sized prawns (shrimp), peeled and deveined
- Pinch of paprika
- 2 tbsp chopped flat-leaved parsley

A more traditional way to cook this tapa is in a flameproof dish called a cazuela, but a frying pan will work fine. Heat the oil in the pan with the garlic and chilli pepper, taking care not to let them burn. Add the prawns (shrimp) and coat with the garlicky oil. Cook the prawns (shrimp) until firm, transfer to a serving dish with the oil and sprinkle with the paprika and parsley.

Aubergine (Eggplant) Dip

The smokiness of the aubergine (eggplant) is crucial in making a good dip, and to get the best effect you'll need to char the skin over a barbecue or under a hot grill (broiler). Serve with plenty of hot pitta bread.

Serves 4

- 2 small or 1 large aubergine (eggplant)
- 3 tbsp olive oil
- 1 tbsp tahini
- Juice of ½ a lemon
- 1 garlic clove, coarsely chopped

Pierce the skins of the aubergine with a fork, then cook over a naked flame (grill or broiler) until the skin chars and the flesh is tender. Leave to cool. Discard the green stems, and peel off the skin completely. Place the aubergines (eggplant) in a blender with the olive oil, tahini, lemon juice and garlic and mix until smooth. Season well.

SALADS

Chorizo Salad

An easy late-night meal. Serve with plenty of crusty bread to mop up the egg and spicy oil from the sausage.

Serves 2

- 2 tbsp olive oil
- ½ large chorizo (about 225 g/8 oz), sliced
- Mixed salad leaves
- ½ sweet red (bell) pepper, seeded and sliced into thin strips
- 4 spring onions (scallions), diced
- Cooked new potatoes, halved (optional)
- 2 free-range hard-boiled eggs
- Handful (about 120 g/4 oz) chopped flat-leaved parsley
- Coarse salt and freshly ground black pepper

Vinegar and Mustard Dressing

- 3 tbsp olive oil
- 1 tbsp red wine vinegar
- Dash of coarse-grain mustard

To make the dressing, whisk together the olive oil and vinegar and add a dash of coarse-grain French mustard. Heat the olive oil and fry the chorizo until lightly browned. Arrange the salad leaves, pepper, spring onions (scallions) and potatoes on two dinner plates or in two pasta bowls. Sprinkle with the chorizo. Shell and quarter the eggs, then carefully place on top of the chorizo salad. Pour the dressing over the salad, season and sprinkle with the parsley.

Panzenella Salad

This Tuscan salad makes use of day-old bread. Use the ripest plum tomatoes you can get, and the most peppery olive oil you have.

Serves 4

- 900 g/2 lb/4 cups ripe tomatoes
- 4 tbsp red wine vinegar
- 150 ml/5 fl oz/$^2/_3$ cup Tuscan extra virgin olive oil
- 2 cloves crushed garlic
- 1 large ciabatta or other white country bread torn into 2.5 cm/1 in pieces
- 2 sweet red (bell) peppers, skinned and sliced
- 1 sweet yellow (bell) pepper, skinned and sliced
- 2 tbsp capers, rinsed
- 2 tbsp pitted black olives
- Large bunch basil, roughly torn

Skin the tomatoes and quarter them. Scoop out the seeds, retaining the tomato quarters, and sieve the seeds into a bowl to squeeze out the juices. Add the vinegar, oil and garlic to the tomato juice and whisk together. Add the bread to the juice and set aside until the juices soak into the bread. Now add the peppers, capers, olives and basil leaves and mix lightly.

Greek Salad

Good flavourful tomatoes are essential to this dish – and try not to keep them in the refrigerator. If you have to, bring them to room temperature before using, as chilling dulls the flavour.

Serves 4

- 4 tbsp peppery Greek olive oil
- 1 tbsp red wine vinegar
- 150 g/5 oz/$^2/_3$ cup feta cheese, diced
- A generous handful black olives (about 150 g/$^2/_3$ cup), halved
- 3 large tomatoes, skinned, seeded and diced
- 1 small or $^1/_2$ large cucumber, diced
- $^1/_2$ sweet red (bell) pepper, seeded and diced
- 1 red onion, thinly sliced into rounds
- 2 tbsp chopped fresh oregano
- Coarse sea salt and black pepper

Whisk together the olive oil and red wine vinegar. In a large salad bowl combine the rest of the ingredients and mix thoroughly with the dressing. Season well.

Beetroot (Beet) and Feta Salad

The white cheese against the stark purple of the beetroot (beet) looks stunning. This dish works equally well with fresh goat's cheese. You'll need a strong, honey-coloured olive oil to finish the dish.

Serves 4 as a starter

- 6-8 beetroot (beets)
- 200 g/7 oz feta cheese, crumbled
- A handful of mint (about 120 g/4 oz), chopped
- A good glug of olive oil (about 125 ml/4 fl oz/½ cup)
- 4 tbsp aged balsamic vinegar
- Coarse sea salt and black pepper

Wash the beetroot (beets), then boil them in their skins until tender. Peel the beetroot, then slice them into 5 mm/¼ in thick rounds. Divide the rounds equally between serving plates, sprinkle with the feta and mint and season to taste. Sprinkle the oil and vinegar over the assembled dishes and serve.

Caesar Salad

Serves 2 as a starter

For the salad

- Olive oil for frying
- 1 large cos (romaine) lettuce, washed and torn into strips
- 2 slices of bread, crusts removed and cut into croutons

For the egg-and-anchovy dressing

- 1 large free-range egg, at room temperature
- 1 garlic clove, peeled
- 3 anchovy fillets
- 2 tbsp lemon juice
- 1 tbsp Worcestershire sauce
- 3 tbsp olive oil
- 20 g/$^{3}/_{4}$ oz parmesan cheese, grated
- Coarse sea salt and black pepper

First make the dressing. Place the egg in a pan of boiling water. Cook for 1 minute, then plunge it into cold water and reserve. When cool, crack the egg into the bowl of a food processor. Add the garlic, anchovies, lemon juice and Worcestershire sauce. Blend well, while slowly pouring in the olive oil. Blend in the grated parmesan. Season to taste. To make the salad, toast the croutons in a frying pan with a little olive oil. Add the lettuce to a serving bowl, pour the dressing over it and mix well. Scatter with the croutons.

Grilled Courgette (Zucchini) and Aubergine (Eggplant) Salad

If you've got the barbecue fired up, don't miss the opportunity to make this impressive side dish.

Serves 6

- 2-3 courgettes (zucchini)
- 2-3 aubergines (eggplant)
- Olive oil to coat
- A handful (about 120 g/4 oz) flat-leaved parsley, roughly chopped
- 2 tbsp pine kernels, lightly toasted
- Olive oil and mustard dressing
- 3 tbsp honey-coloured olive oil
- 2 tbsp lemon juice
- 1 tsp Dijon mustard

Whisk together the ingredients for the dressing until they emulsify. Season and set aside. Slice the vegetables, on the diagonal into no more than 5 mm/¼ in thick slices. Place them in a bowl and coat with the oil, then grill the vegetables on both sides, until they take on the stripes of the hot barbecue. Place them back in the bowl, mix with the dressing, and sprinkle with the parsley and the pine kernels.

Thai Beef Salad

Olive oil is not the first ingredient that springs to mind when you think of Asian cuisine. However, it makes the perfect salad dressing for this Thai salad.

Serves 2

- 2 handfuls (about 250 g/8 oz/1 cup) rice noodles
- 2 ripe tomatoes, diced
- ½ cucumber, seeded and diced
- 2 spring onions (scallions), shredded
- 2 thick steaks, such as rib-eye
- 2 tbsp peanuts, chopped
- Handful (about 120 g/4 oz) chopped fresh coriander
- Coarse sea salt and black pepper

For the spicy dressing

- 1 shallot, finely chopped
- ½ red chilli pepper, seeded and chopped
- 2 tbsp olive oil
- 1 tbsp sesame oil
- 1 tbsp lime juice
- 1 tbsp soy sauce

Whisk together all the ingredients for the dressing and reserve. Cook the noodles in boiling water, pour into a colander and plunge into cold water. Drain well. Place the noodles in a large serving bowl with the tomatoes, cucumber and spring onions (scallions). Pour the dressing over the mixture and mix well. Cook the steaks on a hot grill (broiler) or barbecue until brown on the outside and pink inside. Leave for five minutes to rest, then slice into thin strips. Arrange the beef over the salad, and dress with the peanuts and coriander.

Tricolore Salad

An Italian salad packed with vitamins – and you'll benefit from all the health-giving properties of the extra virgin olive oil when used in its raw state.

Serves 3-4 as a starter (appetizer)

- 3 ripe tomatoes, sliced into rounds
- 2 ripe avocados, peeled, pitted and sliced
- 2-3 rounds of Buffalo mozzarella, sliced
- A handful of shredded basil
- 3 tbsp extra virgin olive oil – a honey-coloured style would be ideal
- 1 tbsp balsamic vinegar
- Coarse sea salt and black pepper

Arrange the tomatoes, avocados and mozzarella on a large serving plate. Scatter over the basil. Whisk together the oil and the vinegar and drizzle over the salad. Season well.

Chick-pea and Cherry Tomato Salad

Fresh herbs, oil and sherry vinegar combine to make this delicious warm salad.

Serves 2 as a side dish

- 3 tbsp olive oil
- 1 red onion, coarsely chopped
- 1 garlic clove, chopped
- 10-12 cherry tomatoes, halved
- 1 x 400 g/14 oz can chick-peas, drained and rinsed
- 2 tbsp sherry vinegar
- A small bunch flat-leaved parsley, chopped, tough stems discarded

---

In a frying pan, heat 1 tbsp of the oil and gently fry the onions so they soften but do not colour. Add the garlic and tomatoes and fry for a further two minutes. Now stir in the chick-peas and heat through. Mix together the vinegar and the rest of the oil, then add to the pan, stirring to coat the chick-peas and tomatoes. Sprinkle with the parsley, season well and serve warm with crusty bread, drizzling a little extra oil over the finished dish.

MAIN COURSES (ENTREES)

 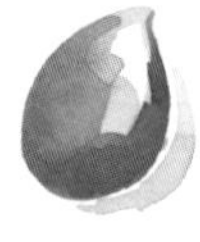  

Monkfish with Lentils

An extremely stylish dinner party main course – it looks impressive but is simple to make. The Italians eat lentils for luck at New Year so try this for a New Year's Eve dinner.

Serves 4

- 4 monkfish tail fillets, membrane removed
- 16 slices Parma ham
- 125 ml/4 fl oz/½ cup olive oil

For the lentils

- 200 g/7 oz Puy (gray) lentils
- 1 stick celery, finely chopped
- 1 onion, finely chopped
- 1 garlic clove, chopped
- 2 tbsp fresh oregano, chopped
- Olive oil for frying
- Coarse sea salt and black pepper

To serve

- 1 lemon, quartered
- 4 tbsp chopped fresh flat-leaved parsley
- Golden lemon-flavoured olive oil

To make the lentils, place the lentils in a large pan with cold water. Bring to the boil, then simmer for around 20 minutes, or until al dente. Meanwhile, fry the celery, onions and garlic until soft. Drain the lentils, then stir them into the celery mixture, along with the oregano. Season well. Pre-heat the oven to 200°C/400°F/gas mark 6. Wrap each of the fish fillets in the slices of Parma ham and place on to a roasting dish. Drizzle generously with olive oil and bake for 20 minutes or until cooked through. Divide the lentils between four deep dinner plates or shallow bowls and place the monkfish on top. Garnish with the lemon wedges and parsley and drizzle with olive oil.

Osso Bucco alla Milanese

Serves 4

- 2 tbsp olive oil
- 25 g/1 oz/2 tbsp butter
- 4 large pieces boned veal shin (about 450 g/2 lb)
- 8 plum tomatoes, skinned
- 2 glasses (225 ml/8 fl oz) dry white wine
- 150 ml/$^1/_4$ pint/$^2/_3$ cup vegetable stock (broth)
- 2 cloves garlic, roughly chopped
- Coarse sea salt and black pepper

Heat the olive oil and butter in a heavy-bottomed casserole dish (Dutch oven) and brown the pieces of veal. Add the tomatoes, white wine, stock (broth) and garlic. Bring to the boil, cover, then simmer for 1$^1/_2$ to 2 hours or until the veal is meltingly tender. Keep an eye on the liquid levels so the pot doesn't boil dry, topping up with water or stock as necessary. Finish with Gremolata (see p111). This dish is usually served with risotto but it is equally delicious with Olive Oil Mash (see p93).

Kleftiko

Legend has it that this Cypriot dish came about because bandits had to prepare their lamb without any smoke being seen, so they'd bury it in a clay pot with hot coals and leave it for 24 hours. Whether that's true or not, sealing the lamb in this way and cooking it slowly with herbs produces a wonderfully aromatic and moist dish. Fortunately, you can use non-stick baking paper and your oven rather than digging holes in the garden!

Serves 4 – 6

- 8 tbsp olive oil
- 1 leg of lamb (about 2 kg/4 lb 8oz)
- 3 cloves garlic, cut into slivers
- Small bunch of thyme
- 4 baking potatoes, cut into thin rounds
- About 125 ml/4 fl oz/½ cup dry white wine
- 2 tsp chopped oregano

Heat a little of the olive oil in a large frying pan and brown the lamb. Using a sharp knife, poke holes in the meat and insert the slivers of garlic and sprigs of thyme. Place the lamb on 2 to 3 large sheets of non-stick baking paper and rub with a little more oil. Tuck the potatoes in around the meat. Add the wine and oregano and season with pepper. Fold the paper over the lamb until you have a loose, yet tightly sealed, parcel. Place on a roasting tray and roast at 180°C/350°F/gas mark 4 for about 2-2 ½ hours or until tender. Remove from the oven and leave to rest for 15 minutes. Slit open the parcel, carve, and serve with the potatoes and juices from the meat.

Gremolata

$^1/_2$ lemon rind
2 fresh bay leaves
1 garlic clove

Grate the lemon rind, ensuring that only the yellow part is used. Then chop the bay leaves and garlic clove finely. You want a mixture to sprinkle over the osso bucco. Traditionally, flat-leaved parsley is used but fresh bay offers a more robust finish to the dish.

Chicken Tagine

The tagine is a traditional Moroccan cooking pot, but a heavy-based pan with a tight-fitting lid will work just as well. Serve this aromatic dish with couscous.

Serves 4

- 8 large chicken thighs, skin on
- Olive oil for frying
- 1 onion, chopped
- 2 cloves garlic, chopped
- 2 carrots, coarsely chopped
- 2 sticks cinnamon
- 2 tsp ground cumin
- 2 tsp ground ginger
- 1 tsp ground turmeric
- About 500 ml/16 fl oz/2 cups chicken stock, enough to just cover the ingredients once in the pan
- 4 tbsp stoned (pitted) green olives
- 1 preserved lemon, sliced
- 4 tbsp chopped coriander (cilantro) to serve

Heat 1 tbsp of the olive oil and brown the chicken in a large saucepan with a lid. The meat is likely to spit so turn the pieces with care. Drain, set aside and drain any excess fat from the pan. Heat 2 tbsp of olive oil in the pan and gently fry the onion, garlic and carrots until they have softened slightly. Add the spices, stir, then return the chicken to the pan. Add the stock, bring to the boil, then cover and simmer gently until the chicken is cooked through and the vegetables have softened – around 45 minutes. Add the olives and the lemon 10 minutes before serving. Sprinkle with the coriander (cilantro) to garnish.

Couscous for Tagine

This is a simple couscous recipe that is an ideal base for a spicy tagine. A common mistake with couscous is to add too much liquid which makes for a heavy dish. The key is not to let it get waterlogged, just have a scant 1 cm/½ in of stock (broth) above the grain when you add the liquid before it is absorbed.

- 200 g/7 oz/1 cup couscous
- ½-¾ stock cube
- 300 ml/½ pint/1¼ cups boiling water
- 1 garlic clove
- ½ lemon, juice squeezed
- 2 tbsp olive oil
- 120 g/4 oz mint leaves
- Coarse salt and freshly ground black pepper

Place the couscous in a medium-sized heatproof serving bowl. Put the stock cube in a measuring jug and add the boiling water. Stir well. Pour the stock over the couscous, cover the dish with aluminium foil and leave for 15 minutes. Crush the garlic clove in a mortar, using a pestle, with a little coarse salt and grind to a paste. Add the lemon juice and oil and mix together, then pour it into a pan and gently heat through. Now, toss the couscous with a fork until light and fluffy. Pour over the garlicky lemon oil, add the mint and season with pepper.

Harissa

Harissa is a spicy sauce from North Africa that peps up dishes such as couscous or grilled meats. You can buy it ready-made – but why bother when it is easy enough to make and tastes so much better fresh? It keeps well in the refrigerator for a week or two in an airtight jar covered with a little olive oil. Be sure to wear rubber gloves when handling the chilli peppers.

Serves 6

- 200 g /7 oz fresh red chilli peppers, seeded and coarsely chopped
- 3 cloves garlic, peeled
- 4 tbsp olive oil
- 1 tbsp tomato purée (paste)
- 2 tsp cumin seeds
- 2 tsp caraway seeds
- 1 tsp coriander seeds
- ½ tsp salt

In a spice grinder or coffee grinder, coarsely grind the cumin seeds, caraway seeds and coriander seeds. Transfer the chilli peppers to a food processor and blend with the rest of the ingredients until you have a smooth paste.

Sausage and Creamy Bean Casserole

A dish inspired by cassoulet, but easier to pull together.

Serves 4

- About 120 ml/4 fl oz olive oil
- 8 Toulouse sausages
- 2 tbsp duck fat (or butter)
- 3 garlic cloves, crushed
- 1 onion, finely chopped
- 2 x 400 g/14 oz cans cannellini beans
- 450 ml / 3/4 pint passata (or unflavoured tomato juice)
- 350 ml/12 fl oz/1 1/2 cups dry white wine
- 1 bouquet garni (2 bay leaves, a few sprigs each of thyme and flat-leaved parsley and a 7.5 cm/3 in celery stick, tied together)
- 50 g/2 oz/1/2 cup dry breadcrumbs
- 120 g/4 oz flat-leaved parsley, chopped
- Coarse salt and freshly ground black pepper

Preheat the oven to 190°C/375°F/gas mark 5. Heat 2 tbsp of the olive oil in a heavy casserole (Dutch oven) and lightly brown the sausages all over. Remove the sausages and reserve them. Heat the duck fat or butter, add the garlic and chopped onion and cook gently, stirring, until softened (about five minutes). Put the sausages back in the pot, together with the beans, passata (tomato juice), wine and bouquet garni. Bring to the boil, then place in the oven. Cook for 1 hour, stirring once or twice. Season to taste. Ten minutes before serving, fry the breadcrumbs and chopped parsley in 2 tbsp of the olive oil over a medium heat, stirring, until lightly toasted. To serve, place the sausages and beans in warm bowls and sprinkle with the toasted breadcrumbs. An extra drizzle of dark green olive oil ups the calorie count but tastes good!

Greek-style Chicken

A simple one-dish meal, that takes minutes to prepare. It takes around 45 minutes to cook, which gives you a chance to unwind with a glass of wine.

Serves 4

- 3 potatoes, skin left on, cubed
- 2 red onions, sliced into rounds
- 2-3 bay leaves
- 3-4 sprigs fresh oregano
- 2 garlic cloves, crushed
- 4 tbsp strong, peppery Greek olive oil
- 8 chicken thighs, skin on
- 1 red pepper, sliced
- 1 sweet yellow (bell) pepper, sliced
- 2 tomatoes, quartered
- 4 tbsp white wine

Preheat the oven to 200°C/400°F/gas mark 6. In a large roasting pan, arrange the potatoes, onions, herbs and garlic, and drizzle with the oil. Roast for 10 minutes, then add the rest of the ingredients. Continue to roast until the chicken is cooked through and the vegetables are soft and slightly caramelized, about 45 minutes. Season well.

Roast Sea Bass with Fennel

Aromatic fennel is a perfect partner to simple sea bass, flavouring its flesh without being overpowering. The fennel must be very thinly sliced or it won't be cooked at the same time as the fish.

Serves 2

- 2 tsp fennel seeds
- 2 whole sea bass, scaled and gutted
- 2 lemons, sliced
- 1 fennel bulb, thinly sliced
- About 125 ml/4 fl oz/½ cup pale lemony olive oil
- 1 small glass (120 ml/4 fl oz/½ cup) dry white wine

Preheat the oven to 190°C/375°F/gas mark 5. Lightly crush the fennel seeds and place them inside the cavity of the fish along with a few slices of lemon. Scatter the fennel slices over the bottom of a large roasting pan, drizzle some oil over them and give the pan a good shake. Pour over the wine, then place the fish on top of the fennel, tucking the remaining slices of lemon on and around the fish. Add a little more oil over the fish and season well. Roast for 30 minutes or so, until the fish is cooked through. Serve with the fennel and a little of the pan juices and an extra drizzle of olive oil.

Grilled, Barbecued and Broiled

There's more to barbecues than burgers, sausages and ribs, good as they can be. The Mediterranean approach makes for a more sophisticated – not to mention much healthier – alternative. Fresh fish and chargrilled vegetables need little more than a sprinkle of extra virgin olive oil to create a sublime alfresco meal. Here are a few ideas on how to compose the perfect Mediterranean grill.

Invest in a large, heavy pestle and mortar – it makes it much easier to knock together marinades and rubs than having to mess around with the food processor.

If you have a charcoal barbecue, try throwing woody herbs, such as rosemary or thyme, on the fire just before cooking. They will release a fragrant smoke that will impart a subtle aroma to your food.

No need to waste your best olive oil basting food – save the extra virgin variety for drizzling over the food just before serving.

Side dishes matter. Unless your guests really want another meatfest barbecue, try and compose a balanced menu just as you would for any other style of eating.

Marinades

Marinating is the classic way to tenderize and imbue grilled food with flavour. Red meat benefits from at least four hours marinating, while more delicately flavoured fish or poultry is generally better when marinated for 1-2 hours. Simply mix all the marinade ingredients together and massage into meat, fish or vegetables.

Rosemary, Garlic and Lemon Marinade

Good with lamb, pork or chicken

- 2 good handfuls fresh rosemary needles, pounded in a mortar
- 4 cloves garlic, crushed
- 8 tbsp olive oil
- 2 lemons, juice squeezed
- Salt and pepper

A Spanish Marinade

Good with lamb and pork

- 2 tsp smoked paprika
- Handful of crushed fresh thyme
- 4 garlic cloves
- 8 tbsp olive oil
- 2 tbsp sherry vinegar
- Salt and pepper

Balsamic Mint Marinade

Good with lamb and vegetables

- 4 shallots, finely chopped
- Bunch of mint
- 6 tbsp balsamic vinegar
- 4 tbsp olive oil
- Salt and pepper

Scallops and Serrano Ham Brochettes (Kabobs)

An elegant appetizer. The trick, as ever with scallops, is not to overcook them.

Serves 6

- 6 wooden skewers
- 24 large scallops, white part only
- 6 slices Serrano ham, cut into strips
- 4 tbsp extra virgin olive oil
- 1 lemon, juice squeezed
- Sea salt and freshly ground black pepper

Soak the skewers in water for 10 minutes to help prevent them from burning on the grill. Rinse the scallops and pat dry. Thread the scallops on to the skewers, interweaving the ham around them like a ribbon. Keep going until you have four scallops and one ribbon of ham on each skewer. Mix the oil and lemon ready for brushing on to the brochettes, and season. Heat the grill to hot. Brush the brochettes generously with the oil and lemon, and place on the barbecue. Grill for 3 minutes, then turn and cook for 3 minutes on the other side. The scallops should be completely opaque. Serve each brochette with a rocket (arugula) salad dressed in a sweet chilli dressing.

Chargrilled Peppers with Anchovies

Serves 6

- 4 sweet red (bell) peppers
- 4 sweet yellow (bell) peppers
- 1 can anchovies in olive oil
- 2 tbsp black olives, stoned (pitted)
- 4 tbsp extra virgin olive oil
- Bunch of marjoram or flat-leaved parsley
- Sea salt and pepper

Place the peppers on a gas grill and char them all over. When suitably blackened, place them in a plastic bag and seal it, the residual heat will complete the cooking. Once peppers have cooled, remove from the bag and rub away the skin. Halve and discard seeds and cores. Sprinkle with the anchovies and black olives. Dress with olive oil, herbs and season with salt and pepper.

Sea Bream in a Fennel Rub

Accompany with Piquant New Potatoes *(recipe on page 133).*

Serves 2

- 2 tbsp fennel seeds
- 1 tsp coarse sea salt
- 1 small garlic clove
- 2 tbsp extra virgin olive oil
- 1 lemon, juice squeezed
- 1 large whole sea bream, scales removed and gutted
- 1 lemon, sliced
- Olive oil for basting
- Coarse sea salt and freshly ground black pepper

To make the rub, pound the fennel seeds with a good pinch of the salt in a mortar with a pestle. When the seeds are well ground, add the garlic clove, oil and lemon juice and pound together to form a paste. Rub this all over the fish, inside and out. Refrigerate for 1-2 hours. Season with salt and black pepper.

Heat the grill to medium (if you are using a charcoal barbecue you may have to experiment with the height of the grill rack). Remove the fish from the refrigerator and place a couple of lemon slices in the cavity. Now you are ready to start barbecuing. Brush the grill rack with oil, then carefully place the fish on it. Baste it regularly with olive oil and move it around from time to time to keep it from sticking – you need to keep the skin intact. Turn the fish after 10-15 minutes to cook the other side. Cooking time will vary between 25 and 35 minutes, depending on your grill and the size of the fish. When done, the flesh will be hot and white, but still moist. Drizzle the fish with extra virgin olive oil before serving – a green, peppery Tuscan oil will do the trick.

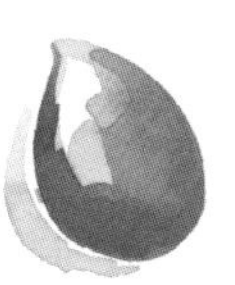
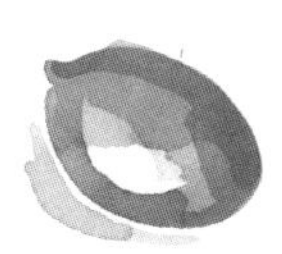

Fresh Tuna Nicoise

Tuna nicoise is often made with canned tuna – and while this is perfectly good, you can turn it into an impressive quick meal by using freshly grilled tuna steaks.

Serves 4

- 4 tbsp olive oil
- 3 tbsp fresh lemon juice
- 1 cos (romaine) lettuce, torn into chunks
- 4 tomatoes, sliced and halved
- 1/2 cucumber, sliced and halved
- 1/2 red onion, thinly sliced
- 6 new potatoes, boiled, halved and cooled
- 120 g/4 oz/1/2 cup sliced green beans, cooked and cooled
- 1 can anchovies in olive oil
- 3 tbsp black olives
- 4 fresh tuna steaks
- 4 free-range eggs, cooked until the yolks are just set
- 50 g/2 oz/1/4 cup fresh basil leaves, torn into small pieces
- Coarse sea salt and freshly ground black pepper

Whisk together the olive oil and lemon juice, and season well with black pepper and coarse sea salt. In a large salad bowl, combine the lettuce, tomatoes, cucumber, onion, potatoes, beans, anchovies and olives. Brush both sides of the tuna with a little oil and, when the barbecue is red hot, add the tuna steaks, searing the marks of the griddle on to both sides of the tuna. Cook for a couple of minutes each side (less if your steaks are thin) so that the fish remains slightly pink in the middle, and transfer to warmed serving plates. Slice the eggs in half and place on top of the salad. Sprinkle with the dressing and then the basil, and serve.

Tagliata

If you want a juicy steak but are in the mood for something quite light, tagliata fits the bill perfectly.

Serves 2

- 2 steaks (preferably rib-eye)
- A little olive oil
- Freshly ground black pepper
- 4 generous handfuls rocket leaves (about 150 g/5 oz/1 1/3 cups)
- 150 g/5 oz parmesan cheese

Olive Oil and Lemon Dressing

- 3 tbsp peppery green olive oil
- 1 tbsp lemon juice

Brush the steaks with olive oil and season with black pepper on both sides. Make the dressing by whisking together the oil and lemon juice.

On a hot barbecue or grill, sear the steaks and cook for a couple of minutes on each side (you can cook the steak for longer, depending on your preference and the thickness of the steaks). Remove the steaks to a warm plate to let the meat rest for five minutes. Scatter the rocket over two serving plates. Slice each of the steaks on the diagonal into 5 mm/1/4 in slices, then arrange on top of the leaves. Pour over the dressing and shave over the parmesan.

Butterflied Lamb

- Leg of lamb
- Balsamic mint marinade (see page 119)
- Salt and pepper

To bone the lamb, first remove the skin. Using a boning knife, slice towards the leg bone, and open the meat out to make a flat slab. Trim if necessary to achieve an even thickness. Place in a shallow dish and rub with the marinade. Leave to marinate for four hours (or ideally overnight). Season the lamb well prior to cooking. Heat on a medium-hot grill, cooking for 10 minutes on each side to get it pink and juicy.

Hamburgers with Red Onion Marmalade

Home-made burgers are easy enough to make and are far better than shop-bought any day. The red onion marmalade adds sweetness and makes a change from tomato ketchup.

Serves 4

For the red onion marmalade

- 3 tbsp olive oil
- 3 red onions, sliced into thin rounds
- 2 tbsp red wine vinegar
- 4 tbsp water
- 2 tbsp soft brown sugar

For the burgers

- 500g /1lb 2oz lean minced (ground) beef
- 1 tsp mustard
- 1 egg, lightly beaten
- 1 onion, finely diced
- A little olive oil
- 4 hamburger buns or ciabatta breads

To make the red onion marmalade, heat the oil in a deep frying pan or sauté pan. Add the onions and fry gently for 10 minutes, stirring frequently. Add the vinegar, water and sugar and cover, cooking gently, for 10 minutes or until the onion has caramelized. Leave to cool. In a large bowl, mix together all the ingredients until well combined. Scoop up a handful of the mixture and shape it into a hamburger. Repeat with the remaining mixture, making sure each burger is roughly the same size. When the barbecue is hot, put the burgers on it and cook for 5-6 minutes each side, depending on how well-done you like them. Serve in lightly toasted hamburger buns with the onion marmalade on the side or on slices of grilled (broiled) ciabatta as an open sandwich.

Barbecued Corn Cobs

Versatile olive oil can be brushed over corn cobs before grilling or broiling, to stop them sticking to the metal bars. It will also help to keep the seasoning in place.

Grilled Halloumi Brochettes (Kabobs)

This robust cheese from Cyprus and Turkey stands up well to the barbecue and is ideal for a vegetarian main dish. If it is not available, use American or Munster cheese.

Serves 3-4

- 1 x 250 g/9 oz package halloumi cheese, cut into bite-size chunks
- 1 sweet red (bell) pepper, seeded and cut into bite-size chunks
- 2 red onions, quartered
- 125 ml/4 fl oz/½ cup olive oil

For the oregano dressing

- 2 tbsp chopped fresh oregano
- 4 tbsp thick, green, peppery olive oil
- 1 tbsp red wine vinegar

If using wooden skewers, soak them in water for 20 minutes or so before use to stop them burning too quickly. Whisk together all the ingredients for the dressing. Thread the cheese, pepper and onions on to the skewers and coat liberally in olive oil. Grill on a hot barbecue until the vegetables have softened. Place on serving plates and pour the dressing over them.

SIDE DISHES

Balsamic Roast Tomatoes

Slow-roasting with a little oil and balsamic vinegar gives the tomatoes a sticky sweetness. Try them with grilled or broiled lamb chops or a steak, or leave them to cool and add them to salad leaves.

Serves 2-3

- 8-10 vine-ripened tomatoes
- 4 tbsp peppery olive oil
- 2 tbsp balsamic vinegar
- 1 tsp sugar
- Coarse sea salt and black pepper
- A good handful of basil leaves (about 120 g/4 oz) torn into small pieces

Preheat the oven to 190°C/375°F/gas mark 5. Quarter the tomatoes and place them in a roasting pan. Pour the oil, vinegar and sugar over them, season generously and give the pan a good shake to make sure the tomatoes get a good coating in the slick of oil. Roast for 30 or so minutes, or until the tomatoes have slightly caramelized. Finish with the torn basil.

Anchovy and Potato Salad

Rather more interesting than the traditional potato salad in mayonnaise.

Serves 4 as a side dish

- 6 large waxy potatoes or 16 salad potatoes, skin left on
- 6 spring onions (scallions), sliced lengthwise into 5 cm/2 in sections
- 12 anchovy fillets
- 3 tbsp olive oil
- 1 lemon, juice squeezed
- 1 small garlic clove, crushed
- Fennel fronds or flat-leaved parsley
- Coarse salt and freshly ground black pepper

Boil the potatoes in salted water to cover. Drain them and, while still warm, but not too hot to touch, peel and chop into 5 cm/2 in cubes. Put the spring onions (scallions) into a salad bowl and add the potatoes. Rinse the anchovy fillets, pat dry and chop roughly. Sprinkle them into the bowl. Prepare a dressing by combining the oil, lemon juice and crushed garlic, seasoned with black pepper and a little salt. Mix all the ingredients together and decorate with flat-leaved parsley or fennel fronds.

Broccoli with Cannellini Beans

Serves 2-4

- 2 tbsp olive oil
- 1 x 400 g/14 oz can cannellini beans
- 1 garlic clove, chopped
- 1 head broccoli, trimmed into florets
- 2 tbsp peppery Tuscan olive oil

Add olive oil to a large pan and stir in the cannellini beans and garlic. Gently heat through. Meanwhile, cook the broccoli in boiling water until it is tender but still firm to the bite. Drain the broccoli and add to the beans. Stir gently to combine. Season and serve drizzled with the Tuscan olive oil.

Garbanzos con Espinacas

A wonderfully tasty Spanish side dish.

Serves 4

- 1 x 400 g/14 oz can chick-peas
- 2 bunches spinach (about 250 g/8 oz/4 cups) shredded, washed, tough stems discarded
- 2 tbsp robust, fruity Spanish olive oil
- 3 garlic cloves, crushed
- 2 slices day-old white bread, crusts removed, cubed
- ½ tsp ground cumin
- ½ tsp paprika
- A pinch of saffron, infused in 3 tbsp hot water

Rinse the chick-peas and drain them. Blanch the spinach in boiling water and drain it, squeezing out any excess water, and set aside. Heat the olive oil in a frying pan, add the crushed garlic, the bread, cumin and paprika and fry until the bread is golden. Place the mixture in a mortar or a blender and grind or mix to a paste. Transfer the mixture back to the pan, stir in the chick-peas, the shredded spinach and the saffron-infused water and heat through.

Healthy Home-fries

Okay, so they're not strictly fries – but they make a very tasty, and much healthier, alternative to the real thing!

Serves 3-4 as a side dish

- 4 large baking potatoes, unpeeled
- 4 tbsp olive oil
- 2 tbsp coarse sea salt

Preheat the oven to 200°C/400°F/gas mark 6. Slice the potatoes lengthwise into eighths. Place them in a large roasting pan, then drizzle with the oil and sprinkle with the salt. Give them a good shake to coat, then roast for around 45 minutes or until they are tender and the skin is crisp. You'll need to turn them every 15 minutes or so, using a metal fish slice (large spatula) or similar.

Ratatouille

This classic French vegetable dish needs a little patience as the vegetables need to be cooked slowly until the flavours mingle. It is delicious served hot with roast pork, but is equally good cold.

Serves 4-6 as a side dish

- 2 large aubergines (eggplant)
- 2 courgettes (zucchini)
- 2 onions
- 2 sweet red (bell) peppers
- 3 tomatoes
- 4 tbsp olive oil
- 2 cloves garlic, chopped
- 1 tsp coriander seeds, lightly crushed
- A handful of basil (about 100 g/3½ oz/½ cup), torn

Cut the aubergines (eggplant) and courgettes (zucchini) into thick rounds and then into cubes. To remove excess moisture, put them in a colander then sprinkle with salt. Put a weighted plate over the top and set aside for 1 hour. Slice the onions into thin rounds, slice the peppers into strips, discarding the seeds, and dice the tomatoes. Rinse the aubergines (eggplant) and courgettes (zucchini) thoroughly under cold running water, then pat dry. Heat the olive oil in a large pan, fry the onions until soft, then add the aubergines (eggplant), courgettes (zucchini), peppers and garlic. Cover and simmer for 30 minutes. Now add the tomatoes and coriander seeds and cook for a further 30 minutes. Finish with the basil.

Mushrooms à la Grecque

A classic mushroom dish that can be served cold as an appetizer or warm as a side dish.

Serves 4

- 3 tbsp water
- 3 tbsp olive oil
- 1 lemon, rind grated, juice squeezed
- 6 coriander seeds, lightly crushed
- 1 bay leaf
- 2 tomatoes, skinned and chopped (optional)
- 250 g/9 oz/2 cups small button mushrooms, cleaned but left whole

---

Add the water, oil, lemon juice, zest, coriander seeds, bay and tomatoes (if using) to a large saucepan. Bring to the boil. Add the mushrooms and simmer for around five minutes. Season. Remove the mushrooms to a serving dish, then bring the sauce to the boil and let it bubble away for a few minutes until you have a thick reduction. Pour the sauce over the mushrooms, stir and serve.

Cumin-roasted Carrots

Far more interesting than a plain boiled carrot is one that is roasted and coated with a scattering of toasted cumin seeds. Try them with roast chicken.

Serves 4 as a side dish

- 4-6 carrots, peeled and cut into 2.5 cm/1 in pieces
- 1 tbsp cumin
- Coarse sea salt and freshly ground black pepper
- About 125 ml/4 fl oz/½ cup olive oil

Preheat the oven to 200°C/400°F/gas mark 6. Place the carrots in a roasting pan and sprinkle with the oil and cumin seeds. Season well, then roast for around 30 minutes or until tender, stirring occasionally.

Broad (Lima) Beans with Feta Cheese

A great summer dish to bring out with barbecued lamb chops.

Serves 4

- 450 g/1 lb/3 cups broad (lima) beans, fresh or frozen
- 200 g/7 oz feta cheese, cut into small cubes
- Small bunch mint (about 75 g/3 oz/⅓ cup), tough stems discarded, roughly chopped

For the garlic and lemon dressing

- 1 small garlic clove
- ½ tsp salt
- 1 lemon, juice squeezed
- 4 tbsp olive oil
- Freshly ground black pepper

Grind the garlic with the salt using a large pestle and mortar until you have a paste. With a fork, whisk in the lemon and oil and season with pepper. Cook the broad (lima) beans, drain them and rinse in cold water. Add them to a serving bowl along with the feta cheese and the mint. Coat well in the dressing, and serve.

Spinach with Lemon and Pine Kernels

For too long, spinach has had a bad press – the stuff of school lunch nightmares, having been boiled down to within an inch of its life! Lightly wilting it in a frying pan and serving it with a little lemon and oil is the way to go – far removed from the soggy green sludge we knew at school. If you don't have pine kernels, try finishing the dish with a sprinkle of freshy grated parmesan instead. You'll need a frying pan with a lid.

Serves 4

- 2 tbsp pine kernels
- 2 tbsp olive oil, plus a little extra for frying
- 700 g/1 lb 8 oz/6 cups fresh spinach
- 2 tbsp fresh lemon juice

Lightly toast the pine kernels in a frying pan with a little oil then set aside. Wash the spinach in two or three changes of water to remove any trace of grit and discard any tough stalks. (Don't worry about draining too much water off the spinach as this will help it cook later.) Heat the olive oil, add the spinach, cover and give the pan a good shake. Return the pan to the heat for a couple more minutes. Remove the lid, season well and sprinkle with the lemon juice and pine kernels.

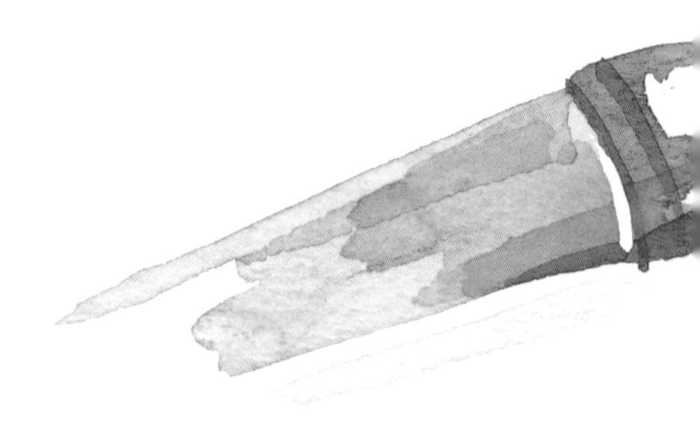

Piquant New Potatoes

Serves 2

- 10-12 waxy new potatoes, skin left on
- 8-10 cherry tomatoes
- 1-2 tsp of chilli pepper flakes
- 2 garlic cloves, finely chopped
- Sea salt
- Black pepper
- 3 tbsp extra virgin olive oil
- Coarse salt and freshly ground black pepper

Cut the larger potatoes in half. Cut the cherry tomatoes in half. Preheat the oven to 190°C/375°F/gas mark 5. Put the oil in a baking pan and place it in the oven for 5 minutes to heat up. Remove the baking pan from the oven and add the potatoes, turning them to coat in oil. Bake for 10 minutes, then scatter with the tomatoes, garlic and chilli pepper flakes (1 tsp for piquant, 2 or more for a spicier taste). Season, stir well and return the pan to the oven. Bake for another 30 minutes, shaking the baking tray from time to time to prevent the tomatoes from sticking.

Baked Fennel with Parmesan

This really is one of those dishes that gets your taste buds working overtime, the combination of sharp lemon and parmesan working perfectly with the aniseed flavour of the fennel. The trick is to bake it until the fennel is quite tender and the parmesan lightly golden. Try it with a pork chop or roast chicken.

Serves 4

- 4 fennel bulbs
- About 450 ml/1 pint/2½ cups vegetable stock (broth)
- 1 lemon, juice squeezed
- 4 tbsp olive oil
- 4 tbsp grated parmesan
- Coarse salt and freshly ground black pepper

Preheat the oven to 190°C/375°F/gas mark 5. Trim the bases of the fennel bulbs. Cut the fennel vertically into 1 cm/ ½ in slices. In a baking dish, layer the fennel and add enough stock to just cover it. Add the lemon juice, and drizzle with oil. Cover the dish with foil and bake for around 40 minutes or until a fork slides easily into the fennel. Remove the foil, increase the oven temperature to 220°C/425°F/gas mark 7 and cook for a further 10 minutes to reduce the liquid a little. Sprinkle with the parmesan and bake for a further 15 minutes or until the cheese is lightly toasted.

Roasted Asparagus with Lemon Dressing

Purists may argue that the only way to eat asparagus is with a generous slick of butter. While we do not disagree, if the oven is hot and you're in the mood for something more robust, try this recipe. A good lemony olive oil is ideal to finish the dish. You can also add a scattering of lightly toasted breadcrumbs.

Serves 4 as a starter

- 2 large bunches fresh green asparagus (allow 6-7 stalks per person)
- 4 tbsp olive oil, plus a little extra for roasting
- Juice of a lemon
- Freshly grated parmesan to serve (optional)
- Coarse salt and freshly ground black pepper

Preheat the oven to 200°C/400°F/gas mark 6. Wash the asparagus and trim off any particularly woody stems. Spread the asparagus in a large roasting pan. Drizzle with oil, giving the pan a shake to coat the asparagus. Roast for around 15 to 20 minutes or until they are tender but still have a little crunch, giving them a shake halfway through the cooking time. Meanwhile, heat the oil-and-lemon mixture gently in a saucepan. When the asparagus is ready, place it on warmed serving plates, pouring the warmed oil-and-lemon mixture over the top. Season generously and sprinkle with the parmesan.

DRESSINGS

Shallot Vinaigrette

This is a delicious dressing for vegetables such as green beans.

- 2 shallots, finely chopped
- 3 tbsp extra virgin olive oil
- 1 tbsp red wine vinegar
- ½ tsp Dijon mustard

Whisk all the ingredients together then leave the flavours to combine for an hour before using.

Classic Mayonnaise

Use a light olive oil for this recipe and combine it with peanut oil so that you don't have too overwhelming a flavour.

Serves 4

- 4 free-range egg yolks
- 1 tsp Dijon mustard
- 1 tbsp lemon juice
- 400 ml/14 fl oz/1½ cups peanut oil
- 150 ml /5 fl oz/⅔ cup light olive oil

Place a large bowl on top of a damp kitchen towel so it won't slip around when you start whisking. Alternatively you can take the easy way out and make it in a blender. Add the egg yolks, mustard and lemon juice and whisk together. Add about 2 tbsp of each of the oils and whisk until they are blended in. Repeat the process, adding the oil gradually until you have the desired consistency. You can vary the proportions of oils, depending on how strongly you want it to taste of olive oil. To make aioli, grind a garlic clove with a little salt into a paste in a mortar with a pestle and add this at the start instead of the mustard – this is delicious with seafood such as lobster or prawns (shrimp).

Sweet Chilli Dressing

12 large, mild, red chilli peppers
6 tbsp extra virgin olive oil
2 tbsp cider vinegar
2 tsp sugar
Salt and pepper

Halve the chilli peppers, seed them and remove the ribs using a teaspoon. Chop the chilli peppers finely – a mezzaluna is handy for this. Place the finely chopped chilli peppers in a bowl and mix in the other ingredients.

Salsa Verde

This robust sauce can be made in advance and goes well with roast lamb but is particularly suited to grilled fish such as salmon or tuna.

Serves 4

- Bunch of flat-leaved parsley (about 120 g/4 oz/½ cup)
- 4 sprigs mint
- 6-8 basil leaves
- 3 tbsp salted capers, rinsed
- 5 anchovy fillets in oil, drained
- 1 garlic clove
- 3 tbsp lemon juice
- ½ tbsp Dijon mustard
- 150 ml/¼ pint/⅔ cup olive oil
- Freshly ground black pepper

Discard any thick stems from the parsley and mint. Put the herbs, capers, anchovies and garlic into the bowl of a food processor, then add the lemon juice and mustard and blend. Add the olive oil gradually and mix until you have a fairly thick sauce. Season with the pepper.

Pesto

Fresh pesto is so very different from even the best shop-bought varieties. It is light, not cloying, and makes a wonderfully simple starter when served with fresh pasta. This pesto is also fantastic served with fresh grilled tuna as a main course.

Serves 2-3 as pasta topping

- 3 large handfuls (about 175 g/6 oz) basil
- 4 tbsp freshly grated parmesan cheese
- 2 tbsp pine kernels
- 1 garlic clove, chopped
- 4 tbsp olive oil
- Coarse salt and freshly ground black pepper
- Serve with about 250 g/8 oz/2 cups cooked pasta

Mix all the dry ingredients in a blender using the pulse setting, then slowly add the olive oil with the blender running. The paste should be lightly mixed rather than a sludge. Season well, and mix with the cooked pasta. You can add a few tbsp of the pasta cooking water if you wish to dilute the pesto a little.

Tomato and Avocado Salsa

A fresh and zingy combination, this salsa goes well with Mexican fajitas or as a side dish to be scooped up with tortilla chips.

- 1 ripe avocado
- 2 tomatoes
- 1/2 red onion
- 1/2 red chilli pepper, seeded and finely chopped
- Small bunch of fresh coriander (cilantro), washed and chopped
- 1 lime, juice squeezed
- 2 tbsp olive oil
- Coarse salt and freshly ground black pepper

Chop the avocado, tomatoes and onion into medium dice. Place in a serving bowl and stir in the chilli pepper, coriander, lime juice and oil. Stir well and season to taste.

AND FOR DESSERT…

Using olive oil in baking produces a wonderful moist cake. Choose a mild-flavoured variety as you don't want it to taste too powerful.

- 400 g/14 oz/1½ sticks unsalted butter
- 400 g/14 oz/1½ cups golden caster sugar or light brown sugar
- 6 eggs
- 2 tbsp light olive oil
- 150 g/5 oz/⅔ cup ground almonds
- 500 g/1 lb 2 oz/2 cups yellow cornmeal
- 2 lemons, rind grated, juice squeezed
- 1 tbsp vanilla essence (extract)
- Icing (confectioner's) sugar for dusting

Preheat the oven to 180°C/350°F/gas mark 4. Grease a 23 cm/9 in springform cake tin (pan) and line it with non-stick baking paper. Put the butter and sugar into a large bowl and beat thoroughly until creamed. Add the eggs gradually, and mix thoroughly. Stir in the olive oil. Fold in the rest of the ingredients, taking care not to over-mix. Pour the mixture into the prepared cake tin (pan), and spread evenly. Bake for around 30 minutes or until the top is lightly golden. Dust with icing (confectioner's) sugar. Serve with the balsamic strawberries (see next recipe).

Balsamic Strawberries

Balsamic vinegar really enhances the flavours of the fruit.

- Large punnet (about 350 g/12 oz/1¾ cups) strawberries, hulled and sliced
- 2 tbsp caster (superfine) sugar
- 1 tbsp balsamic vinegar
- 1 tbsp chopped mint

Combine all the ingredients in a large bowl, except the mint, and leave to marinate for 30 minutes. Decorate with the mint.

Olive oil for health

The use of olive oil as a medicine stretches way back and it was widely used in ancient Greece to treat all manner of ills. Greek physician Hippocrates, known as the 'father of medicine', listed more than 60 medical uses for the oil, treating everything from dermatological problems and ulcers to burns and infections. Even before that, Hippocrates' teacher Herodicus advocated the use of olive oil as a muscular massage for Olympic athletes.

It was not just the oil that was used in medicine – the leaf, too, has been much lauded. Writing in the *Pharmaceutical Journal* in 1854, British physician Daniel Hanbury discussed his success in combatting fevers with the leaf. He would boil the leaves and use the liquid to treat people stricken with fever and malaria, and he speculated that a bitter substance in the leaves was the active ingredient. This was later named oleuropein, and a great deal of research is under way into how to utilize its anti-viral and anti-bacterial properties, which could treat a wide range of conditions including HIV.

Today, it is widely accepted that the olive – particularly the oil – can provide a number of health benefits. Yet there is no definitive answer as to what makes the fruit so effective.

The Mediterranean Diet

In the 1950s it was observed that people in the Mediterranean, particularly those in Crete, lived longer and had a lower incidence of chronic diseases than people elsewhere. Their diet consisted of an abundance of fruits, vegetables and cereals; little meat was eaten and wine was consumed in moderation. They also used olive oil as their main source of fat.

Today, it is widely accepted that the olive – particularly the oil – can provide a number of health benefits

Much research has been undertaken to try to determine why this diet has a number of health benefits, whether it is one magical ingredient alone or whether it is the diet in its entirety, along with certain lifestyle factors, that is responsible. Many studies have focused exclusively on olive oil and whether this is the magic bullet.

There has been a particular focus on olive oil and its contribution to heart health. One study, for example, looked at the power of phenols in olive oil, which have anti-inflammatory, antioxidant and clot-preventing properties. It was found that the blood vessels of test subjects who had olive oil with a high content of phenolic compounds could dilate better, which could improve blood flow. Similar studies after high-fat meals such as a burger and fries showed impairment of normal blood vessel functions.

Other work has looked into whether olive oil can prevent cancer. American researchers showed in a laboratory that oleic acid, the main monounsaturated fatty acid contained in olive oil, can cripple a certain cancer gene that is responsible for 25 to 30 per cent of all breast cancers. Another laboratory test concluded that phenols extracted from the oil could safeguard against colon cancer or stop the cancer from spreading.

A team of UK researchers looked at the incidence of bowel cancer in 28 countries and found that those who ate a lot of meat and fish, as opposed to those who ate mostly vegetables and cereals, were at increased risk of the disease, and that a diet rich in olive oil was associated with a decreased risk. The team showed that olive oil seemed to reduce the amount of bile acid and increase diamine oxidase levels, which could protect against abnormal cell growth. An experiment on rats also found that an olive oil diet could prevent the development of bowel cancer. Several studies have linked olive oil and other sources of monounsaturated fat to a lower risk of breast cancer.

Several studies have linked olive oil to a lower risk of breast cancer

Chewing the fat

According to the Harvard School of Public Health, detailed research shows that the total amount of fat in the diet, whether high or low, isn't actually linked with disease and what really counts is the type of fat in the diet. Bad fats, namely saturated and trans fats, increase the risk of certain diseases, while good fats – monounsaturated and polyunsaturated fats – lower the risk.

Sources of saturated fat include animal fats, cream, cheese and butter, while monounsaturated fats are found in oils such as olive oil and peanut oil. Polyunsaturated fats are found in oils such as sunflower and corn. Trans fats, in the form of hydrogenated oils, are now generally accepted to be bad for you when it comes to heart health. Such fats are added to products such as bakery items and dairy products to give them a longer shelf life.

Olive oil is often cited as the best choice when it comes to managing cholesterol levels. Cholesterol is essential for the formation of cell membranes, some hormones and vitamin D, but too much of a certain type of cholesterol can lead to heart disease.

It is reckoned that, in moderation, olive oil can lower LDL (bad cholesterol) without affecting HDL (good cholesterol). Saturated fats are said to raise the bad cholesterol and lower the good cholesterol, some polyunsaturated oils can reduce levels of both HDL and LDL, whereas monounsaturated oils reduce only the bad cholesterol.

Following the results of substantial research, olive oil in the US can now carry a label citing its health benefits. In 2004, the US Food and Drug Administration evaluated all the available evidence and announced that olive oil, and certain products containing it, could carry the following claim: 'Limited and not conclusive scientific evidence suggests that eating about 2 tablespoons (23 grams) of olive oil daily may reduce the risk of coronary heart disease due to the monounsaturated fat in olive oil. To achieve this possible benefit, olive oil is to replace a similar amount of saturated fat and not increase the total number of calories you eat in a day.'

Olive oil is often cited as the best choice when it comes to managing cholesterol levels

By replacing the 'bad' fats that you consume with 'good' fats, you will be doing your diet a big favour – as long as you're not increasing your overall fat intake.

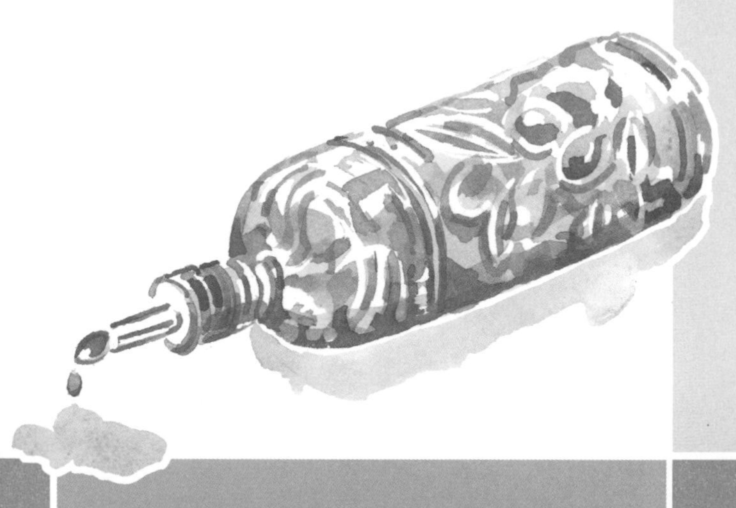

The benefits of olive oil have also been investigated for other health conditions:

Olive oil as a painkiller
According to a recent study, olive oil could act as a natural painkiller. A team of US researchers discovered that a compound in the oil – oleocanthal – acts in a similar way to anti-inflammatory painkiller ibuprofen, affecting the same chemical pathways.

The team found that 50 g/2 oz of extra virgin olive oil was equivalent to about a tenth of a dose of ibuprofen and, while the effect was not strong enough to ease headaches, it could explain the effectiveness of the Mediterranean Diet. The health benefits of the olive-oil-rich diet, such as decreasing the likelihood of heart disease and strokes, are also associated with certain drugs such as aspirin and ibuprofen.

Olive oil and diabetes
Olive oil may also help in controlling diabetes or delaying its onset, as it helps control blood sugar levels.

Olive oil and bone health

Olive oil appears to aid calcium absorption, and so it is helpful in preventing osteoporosis.

Olive oil and cognitive function

A study of olive-oil-rich diets in healthy elderly people found they were less likely to suffer age-related cognitive decline, although it is not known exactly why. One possible explanation put forward is that it is because the monounsaturated fatty acids help to maintain the structure of the brain cell membranes. A high intake of monounsaturated fatty acids appear to protect against age-related disorders – in particular, memory loss and mental declines.

Olive oil and blood pressure

Various studies have shown that olive oil consumption can help reduce blood pressure levels, and could reduce the need for daily blood pressure medications.

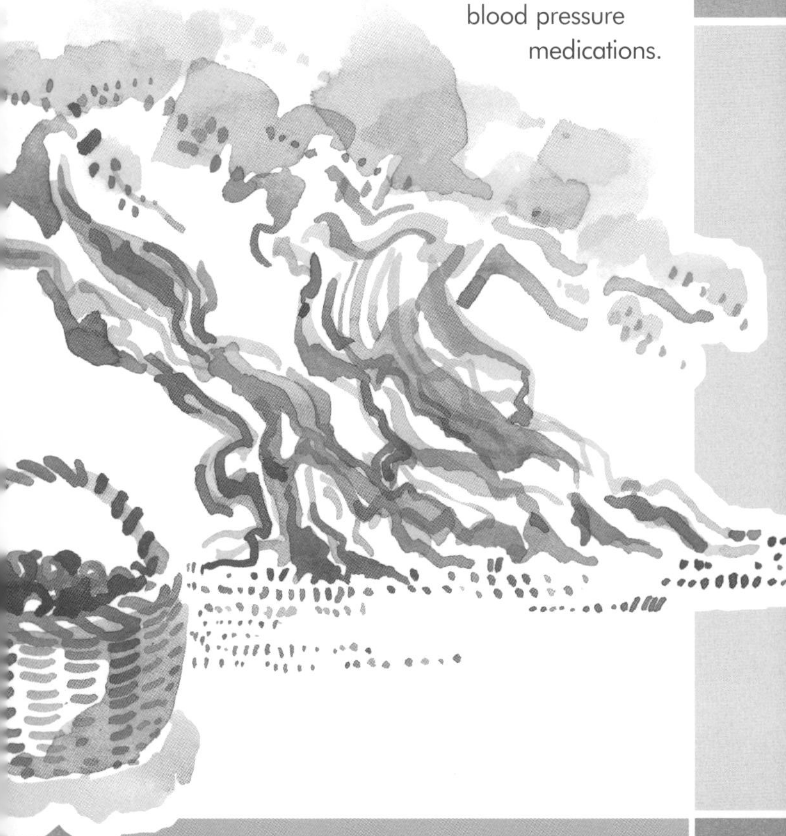

Get fresh

It is important to note that many of these health benefits are associated with fresh extra virgin olive oil. How it is stored, how it is processed, and for how long, can all affect the levels of valuable compounds in the oil. It is also much debated whether or not heating the oil can diminish some of its valuable properties. So, if you want to ensure you're getting the most out of your oil in terms of health, use it young, dash it on in its natural state over your salad or use it in place of butter on fresh bread!

Olive oil and rheumatoid arthritis

It is believed that olive oil has an anti-inflammatory effect that could benefit people with rheumatoid arthritis. A study found that supplementing the diet with olive oil could reduce the number of painful joints, improve grip strength and reduce the length of time that the patients had stiff joints. Another body of research found that the lifelong consumption of olive oil and cooked vegetables protected people from the development of the condition. Those in the highest category of olive oil consumption had approximately one third of the risk of developing rheumatoid arthritis compared to those in the lowest category of olive oil consumption.

Olive oil for virility

Olive oil is a good source of vitamin E – widely credited as the 'fertility vitamin'. This was a fact not lost on the ancient Greeks who ate olives as an aphrodisiac.

Olive oil and longevity

French woman Jeanne Calment lived to the ripe old age of 122 and credited her longevity to olive oil, port wine and chocolate. Not only did she consume the oil, she also used it on her skin.

What's in olive oil?

It is important to remember that olive oil is still a high-fat food – a tablespoon contains 120 calories, the same as other liquid oils. However, it is believed to be healthier than other fats because 77 per cent of the fat is monounsaturated. Olive oil is also packed with antioxidants, which include vitamin E, carotenoids and phenolic compounds. Don't be misled by olive oil labelled as 'light' as this only refers to the flavour and not a lower calorie or fat content.

Olive oil for beauty

The ancient Greeks revered olive oil – not only for culinary use but for what it could do to beautify the body. Athletes in the Olympics performed naked to demonstrate their well-honed physiques and they prepared their bodies with oil beforehand.

Romans were ardent believers in the powers of the oil, and it was used in bathing and creating scented ointments, and to moisturize

The oil would have been mixed with sand as protection from the sun and to regulate body temperature. After the event, the oil, sand and sweat would be removed with a special curved instrument called a strigel. Women also relied on the oil to beautify themselves, using it to condition both skin and hair. Romans, too, were ardent believers in the powers of the oil, and it was used in bathing, and creating scented ointments, and to moisturize.

These ancient civilizations' insights into how olive oil could be utilized hold valuable lessons for beauty routines today. Olive oil is the opposite of what is typically on offer on the shelves of our cosmetics stores. It is pure, chemical-free and natural, providing us with a gentler beauty treatment than the highly processed, additive-laden products that make up a large proportion of today's cosmetics market. Look at the back of an everyday hair conditioner, for example, and you will see a long list of chemicals that help give you that 'salon shine'.

With allergies on the increase and concerns about how these chemicals may affect us long term, many consumers are looking for more natural alternatives. Fortunately, you don't have to look too far, as much of what you need is sitting in the kitchen cupboard, with olive oil taking centre stage.

You won't need much of the oil for the beauty treatments we suggest, as a little goes a long way, so buy a good quality extra virgin oil to ensure you're putting the purest ingredients on to your body.

Beauty tips

- Sophia Loren is a big fan of olive oil. The Italian actress, who at 71 was voted the world's most naturally beautiful person, puts her looks down to her love of life, spaghetti and the odd bath in virgin olive oil. So, add a few drops to running water for silky smooth skin.

- Use it as a conditioner. Gently warm a small cup of olive oil and massage it into your hair, paying particular attention to the ends, and massaging it into your scalp if it is particularly dry. Cover your hair in a plastic bag or an old shower cap and leave for 30 minutes. Rinse thoroughly and shampoo if necessary. You can also rub a few drops over dry hair to eliminate frizz.

- Another home-made conditioner you can try uses a combination of honey, oil and egg. It sounds like a sticky mess but it does work and will leave you with lustrous locks. You'll need one

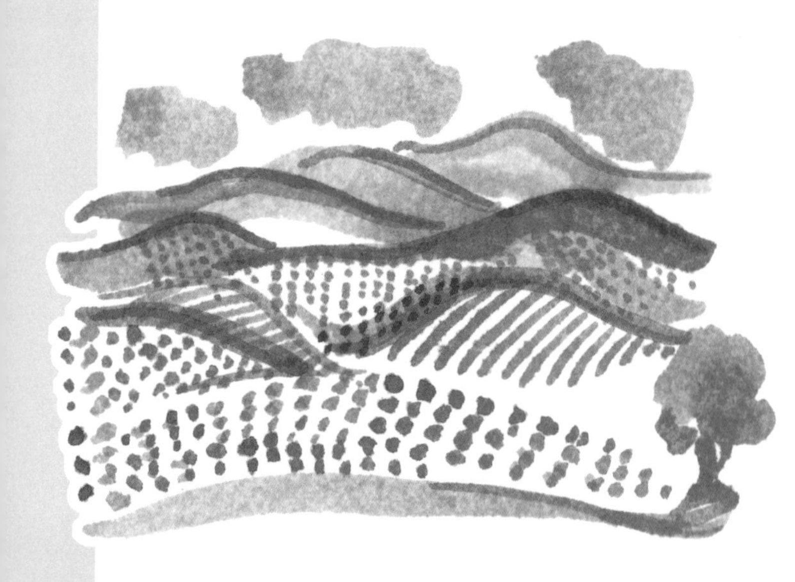

teaspoon of honey, two tablespoons of oil and an egg yolk. Mix the ingredients together and massage into the hair. Wrap your hair in a plastic bag and leave for 20 minutes, before rinsing and shampooing.

- If you run out of shaving foam, use a little olive oil instead. It will make your razor glide over the skin smoothly.

- Olive oil acts as a very effective cleanser. Add a little to cotton wool and wipe gently over the face.

- If your hands or feet are particularly dry, rub some oil into them overnight. Wear gloves or socks so that it doesn't transfer to your bedding.

- Use olive oil as a nail strengthener and cuticle softener. Add the oil to a small bowl and soak your nails for half-an-hour each week, or use before pushing your cuticles back. You can re-use the oil several times for this purpose, so it is not as extravagant as it might sound.

- Massaging with olive oil has been used throughout the ages to help reduce stretch marks.

- This beauty tip is particularly good for gardeners. If your hands are looking somewhat the worse for wear, mix a teaspoon of sugar or coarse sea salt with the same of olive oil and massage it over your hands for a few minutes, then rinse.

- You can make a number of face masks with olive oil. Mix a few drops of oil with one teaspoon of egg yolk and one teaspoon of honey. Spread on to the face and leave for 15 minutes, then rinse. Or you can mash an avocado with a tablespoon of oil, apply to the face, leave for ten minutes and rinse – this is particularly good if you have dry skin.

- For rough elbows, cut two lemons in half, make a little hole in the middle of each, pour in a little olive oil, then rest your elbows in them for 15 minutes. It might look a little bizarre but it is effective.

- Buy an attractive storage bottle for your olive oil so you can keep it in the bathroom rather than dragging your big kitchen stash out each time – but only store a small amount, as olive oil reacts adversely to heat and light.

Home tips

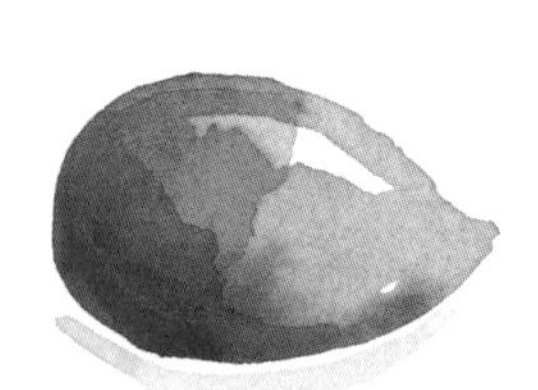
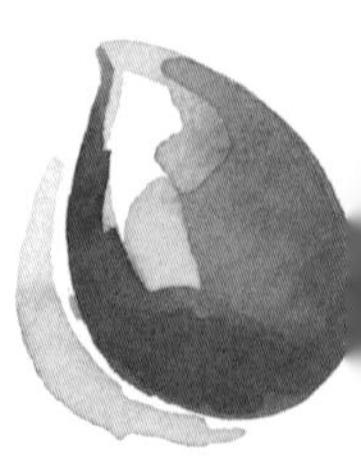

Olive oil has numerous uses around the home and, if you're concerned about all the strong chemicals we use every day, it offers a more natural alternative.

- Add some olive oil to a soft cloth to shine up tired water-marked wooden furniture. The stains disappear and the wood will take on a nice gleam. You can also make your own furniture polish by mixing one part lemon juice with two parts of olive oil. Pour it into a spray bottle for easy use.

- You can remove chewing gum from hair with a little oil. Rub into the affected strands until the gum can be separated.

- Use olive oil to remove paint from your hands. If there's a lot of paint that is tough to shift, mix the olive oil with a little coarse salt first.

- Rub a little olive oil over wooden chopping boards and salad bowls to condition them and prevent cracking.

- If your chamois leather has gone dry and stiff, soak it in water with a spoonful of olive oil.

- Olive oil can be used to remove tar. Let the oil soak in and then the tar will be easier to remove.

- Olive oil has long been used as a sexual lubricant. Today, some people swear by it as a natural aid but the medical profession is out on this one – especially if being used with condoms as it can actually damage the rubber.

Body tips

Olive oil also forms part of the medicine cabinet:

- Medical professionals often recommend using a few drops of warmed olive oil to help soften ear wax before having it syringed.

- Olive oil is gentle and effective for treating constipation, when it is usually mixed with orange or lemon juice. Mix together a teaspoon of oil and a teaspoon of juice.